TABLE OF CONTENTS

Feature Story: 18-Hour Cities

In the U.S., 24-hour cities essentially translate to our gateway cities: Boston, Chicago, Los Angeles, New York, San Francisco, and Washington D.C. Meanwhile, 18-hour cities are the markets with above-average urban population growth, plus a lower cost of living and lower cost of doing business relative to those 24-hour cities. The poster children for this emerging class of up-and-comers have been cities like Denver, Austin, and Nashville.

Although new markets and metros are always on the rise, in 2017 we predicted that the next 18-hour cities would be Milwaukee, WI, Columbus, OH, Charleston, SC, and Kansas City, MO. We identified these four cities because they generally have had population and employment growth well above the national rate, major millennial migration and influx of institutional capital—all key factors in how our Investments team assess potential growth in a metro area.

So how have these markets actually performed since 2017? Taking a high level look at the ULI (Urban Land Institute) U.S. Markets to Watch rankings, Milwaukee and Kansas City have improved the most overall, but Charleston and Columbus have also grown for the better.

Market	What We Liked in 2017[1]	Performance Since 2017
Milwaukee, WI	• New development • High 5-year millennial growth	• Low cost of living and doing business • Introduction of new public transit and new NBA stadium
Columbus, OH	• Above national average employment growth • Home to one of the nation's largest universities	• Relative low cost of living and rapidly growing population • Low unemployment rate • Diverse economic base
Charleston, SC	• Year-over-Year population growth growing at approximately double the national rate • Downtown vibrancy	• Employment has grown at nearly twice the national average for the past five years • Growing sales volume • Companies relocating and expanding
Kansas City, MO	• Above average employment growth • Rise of technology • Affordability	• Expanding biotech & telecom hub • Business friendly environment

[1] Source: PwC and the Urban Land Institute: Emerging Trends in Real Estate® 2019. Washington, D.C.: PwC and the Urban Land Institute, 2018.

Market Overview & Comparison

We measured the performance of these cities based on four major factors:

1. Millenial Population (%)[2]
2. Employment Growth[3]
3. Cost of Doing Business & Affordability Index[4]
4. Influx of Institutional Capital[5]

MILLENIAL POPULATION (%)

Buying a home in a 24-hour city is simply not in the budget for most millennials, so young workers are relocating in search of well paying jobs, affordable housing, and a live-work-play balance. As the largest cohort of the workforce, millennial migration greatly impacts the employment growth of an area as they move in.

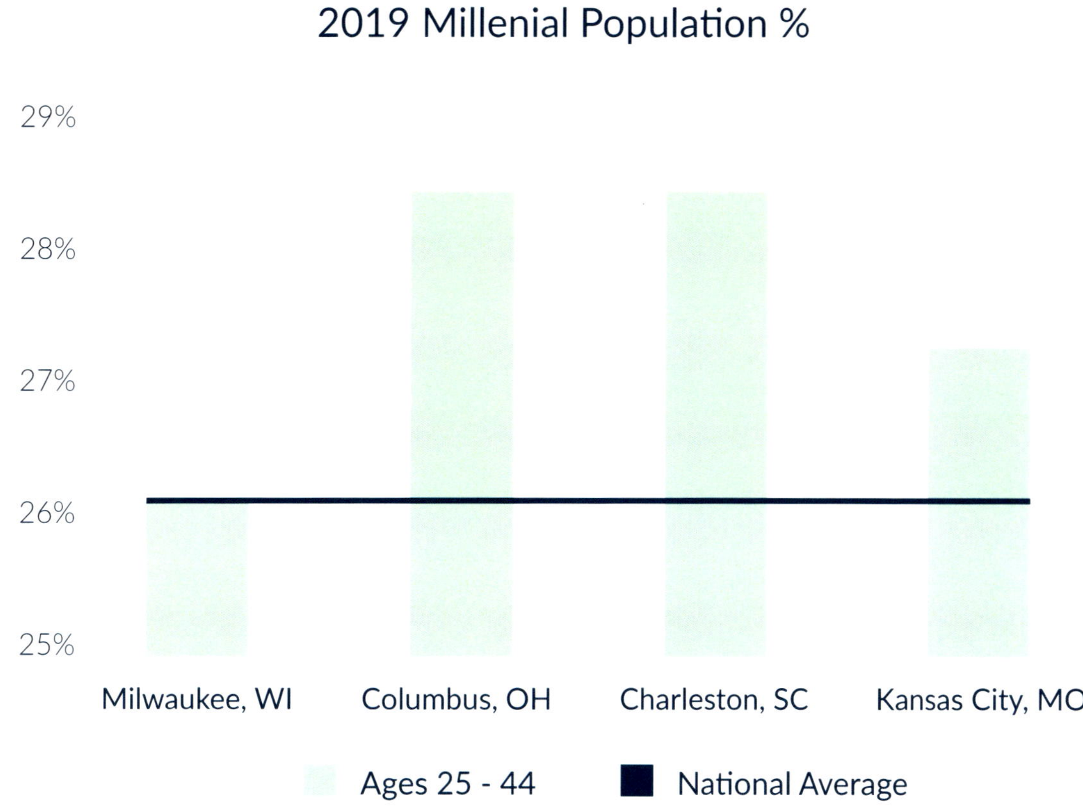

Of the four up-and-comers, Columbus and Charleston are the cities that stand out with a higher than average millennial population.

[2] Source: PwC and the Urban Land Institute: Emerging Trends in Real Estate®2019. Washington, D.C.: PwC and the Urban Land Institute, 2018.
[3] Source: Bureau of Labor Statistics (April 2019)
[4] Ibid [2]
[5] Source: Real Capital Analytics (July 2017-July 2019)

EMPLOYMENT GROWTH

Employment growth indicates a market's economic health, and gives us insight to employers' confidence in the market. Employment growth can also be used as an indicator of future growth. Charleston greatly outperformed the competition, growing at nearly double the national average growth rate.

5- Year Average Annual Employment Growth

Charleston: 2.9%

Columbus: 1.8%

Kansas City: 1.7%

Milwaukee: 0.9%

USA: 1.6%

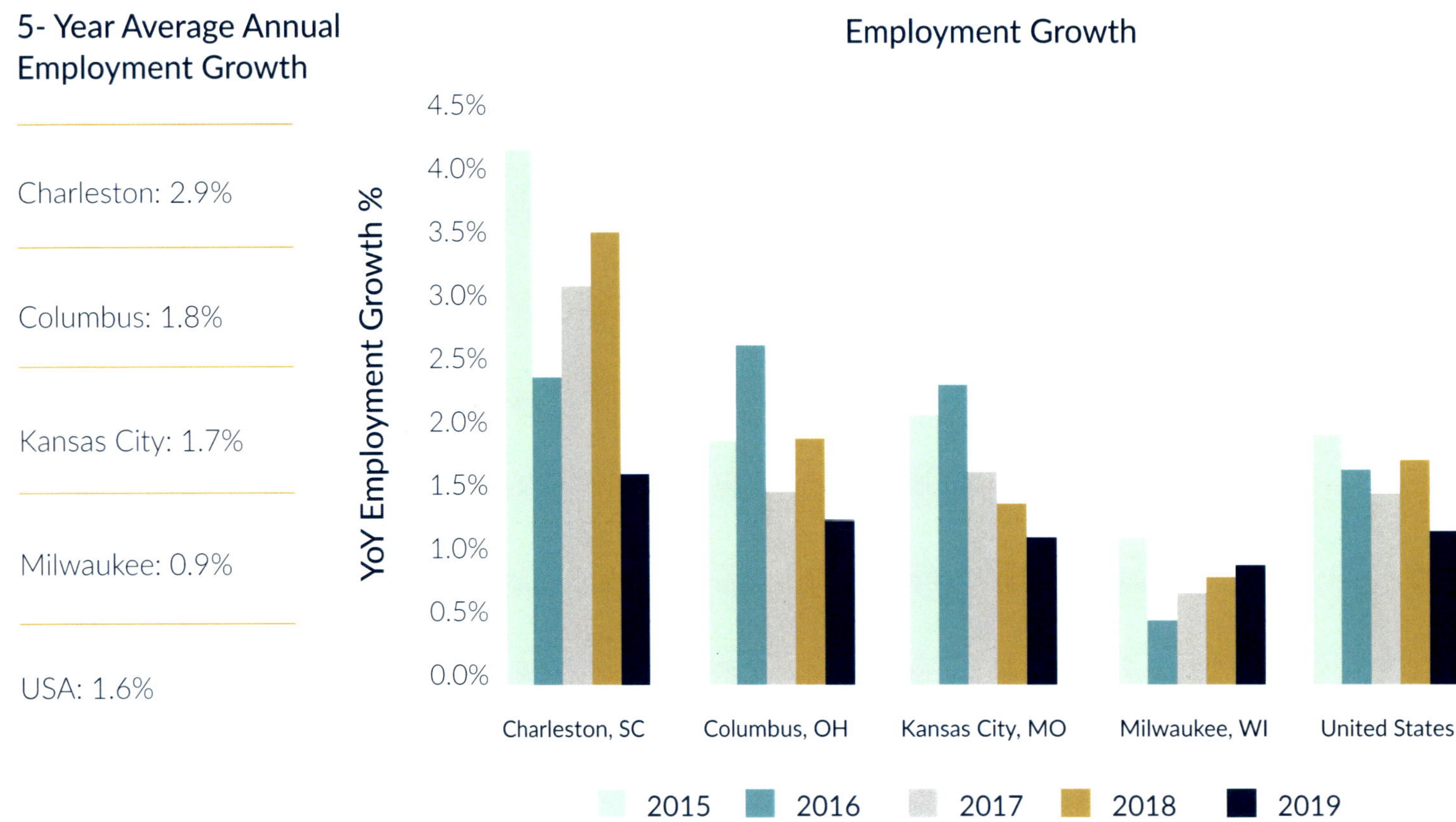

COST OF DOING BUSINESS & AFFORDABILITY INDEX

Location	2019 Cost of Doing Business	2019 Cost of Living/ Affordability Index[6]
Milwaukie, WI	96.3	153.1
Columbus, OH	94.3	196.2
Charleston, SC	98.4	137.9
Kansas City, MO	95.4	193.2
United States of America	100.0	151.7

[6] The affordability index is measured by the percentage of residents that can buy a home at the median home price with the median income for the market.

Cost of doing business can be vital to a market's success as some companies will choose to forgo one market in lieu of a cheaper neighboring market, like Chicago-area companies moving to Milwaukee.

INFLUX OF INSTITUTIONAL CAPITAL

Institutional capital represent investments made from pension funds, endowments, foundations, etc. They represent where the 'big money' is moving. Columbus had the largest influx of institutional capital in a 24 month period from July 2017-July 2019 with nearly $2 billion (B) in institutional investment, making it the closest in institutional capital akin to the golden-child 18-hour city of Nashville.

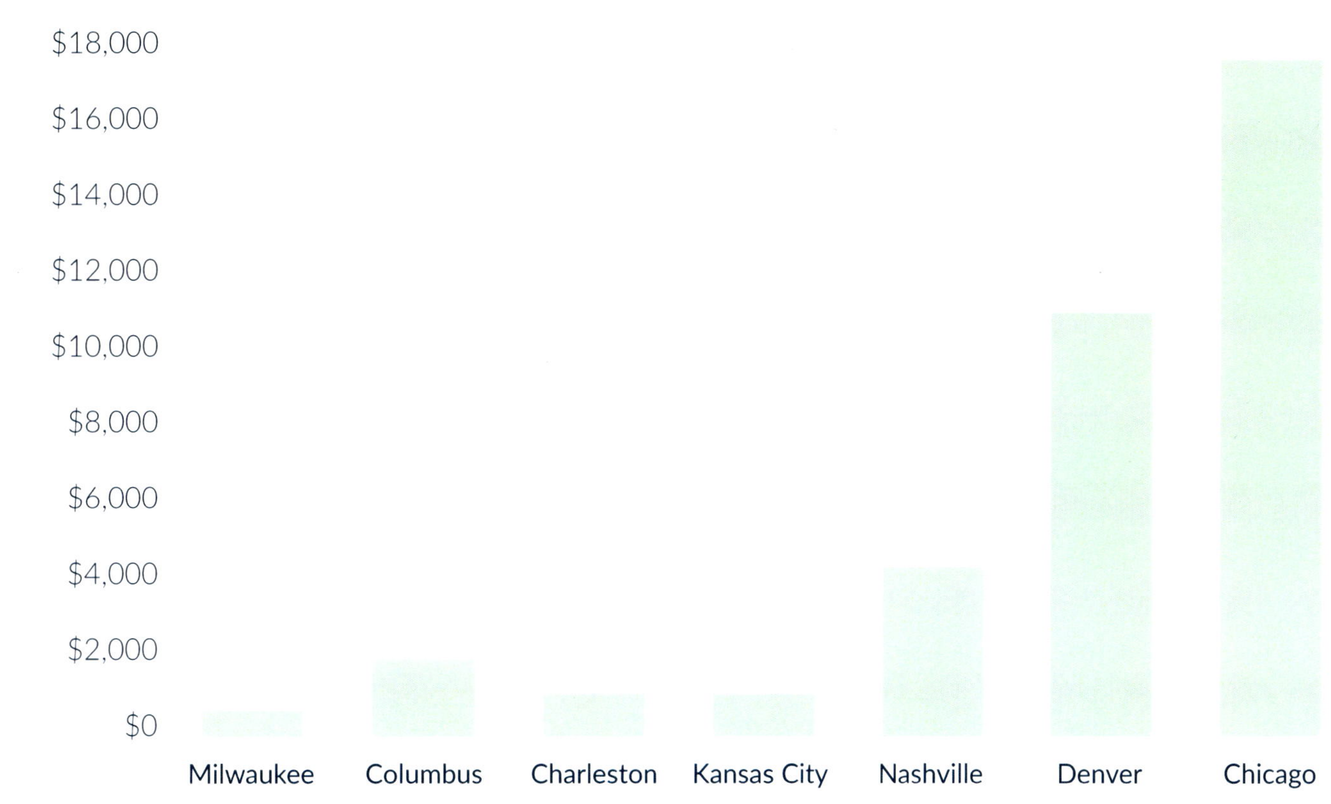

[7] Institutional Capital sales volume was pulled from Real Capital Analytics on July 16, 2019.

City Breakdown

MILWAUKEE

Milwaukee was chosen as an up-and-coming 18-hour city in large part due to the amount of major development projects underway/completed. One of the largest projects of 2018 was the $524 million (MM) Wisconsin Entertainment and Sports Center, home of the Milwaukee Bucks NBA team. Another large project is the new streetcar, named The Hop, which will run downtown within a quarter mile of the most densely occupied office towers.

One of the largest office towers in Milwaukee is also home to one of the city's most recognized companies, Northwestern Mutual. Regardless of the recently announced hiring freeze within the metro area, they remain committed to the city and have invested $450MM in their headquarters in the downtown core.

Milwaukee also has a lower cost of doing business, especially in comparison to its neighboring 24-hour city, Chicago. Several companies have already made the journey north from Chicago to Milwaukee, including Gold Standard Banking (bringing 300 jobs), Vonco Products, and Colbert Packaging.

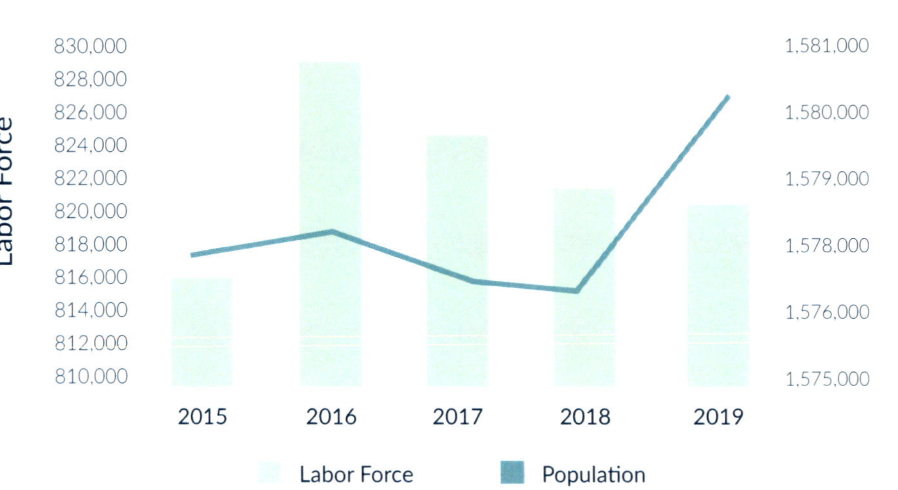

Milwaukee's manufacturing employment comprises 14.3% of the labor force, nearly double the national average. As automation continues to improve, the city's exposure to manufacturing jobs could negatively affect employment

[8] Total Sales Volume & Supply Source: CoStar Q1 2019

[9] Labor Force Source: Bureau of Labor Statistics (April 2019) Population Growth Source: CoStar

growth. However, the city is taking steps in order to reduce that exposure through non-profit programs. The Milwaukee Economic Development Corporation offers technical training and financial assistance to companies dedicated to growing their business in Milwaukee. More generally, Wisconsin as a whole is incentivizing businesses to relocate with tax incentives including exemptions, credits, and other preferential treatment.

While Milwaukee hits the mark of an up-and-coming 18-hour city with its relative low cost of doing business and rising population, it falls a bit short on employment growth and the influx of institutional capital. As some of the metrics are a mixed bag, we will continue to watch Milwaukee's progress.

COLUMBUS

Most notably, Columbus' labor force and population have grown tremendously and don't seem to be slowing. Positive net migration, specifically college-educated millennials moving to downtown Columbus, has aided the population growth.

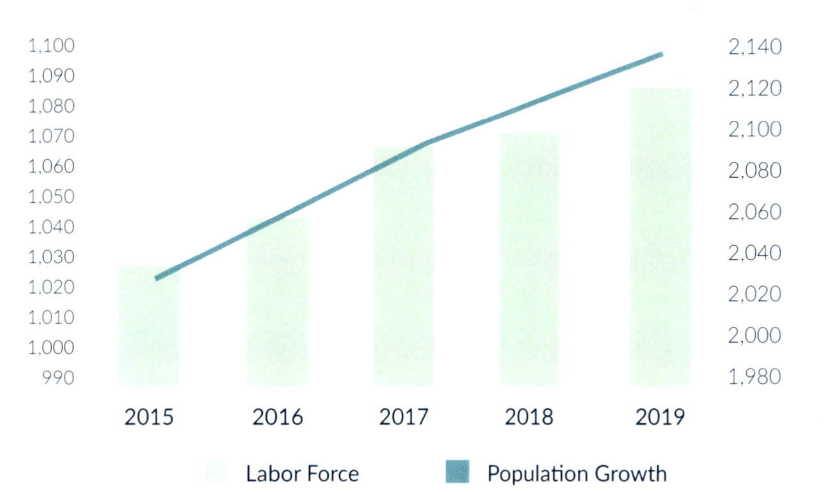

Due to the millennial migration, Columbus has a higher than average population of prime workers (employees ages 25-44). As the labor market is extremely tight with unemployment below 3.0%, the influx of quality workers is welcomed.

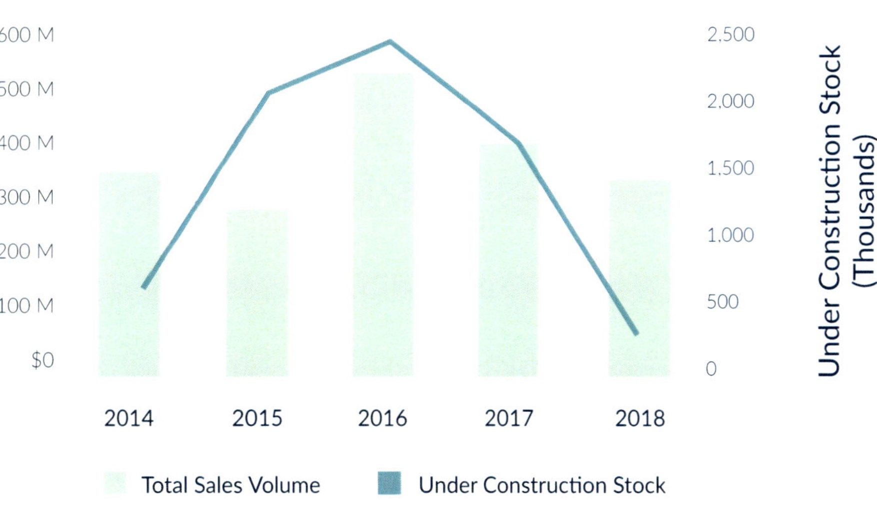

Unlike other midwest cities, Columbus doesn't have a large exposure to manufacturing, shielding it from potential job loss due to automation. Alternatively, a large portion of the labor force, 16% of overall employment, is employed by the state government, providing a sturdy backbone and less office rent volatility. Sector diversity within an economy provides insulation against economic volatility. Other expanding sectors in Columbus include education, healthcare, professional services, and hospitality.

Approximately 7,800 multifamily units are currently under construction, with a majority of projects within the downtown core. Despite the boom in construction, multifamily vacancy remains near record lows at 6.1%. Net absorption (the amount of space that was occupied) was positive as over 3,000 apartments were occupied from June 2018 - June 2019, rounding out the extremely healthy fundamentals. Columbus has also had a push of development in the past two years. Over 2.5 million square feet (MSF) of office space delivered, more than the previous ten years combined.

CHARLESTON

We chose Charleston as an 18-hour city due to its downtown vibrancy, population and job growth. Charleston has continued to build on that momentum and can be characterized by low unemployment, strong net migration, and investor demand.

Sales volume hit a record high in 2018 as 200 office buildings traded for a total of $330 MM, beating a record year in 2017. Sales volume in 2019 is likely to continue on an upward trajectory.

Economically, Charleston is booming as employers are flocking to the area to expand, following the likes of Boeing and Mercedes-Benz, to name a few. Charleston's average five year job growth of 2.9% is nearly double the national average of 1.6%. According to the Chamber of Commerce, 9,000+ jobs were created in 2018 alone and Vovlo recently expanded into a $1.1B factory that will hire on an additional 4,000 employees.

The Port of Charleston has also been a driving force in expanding job growth, specifically manufacturing jobs. The Port's deepening of the Charleston Harbor will accommodate increased container volume.

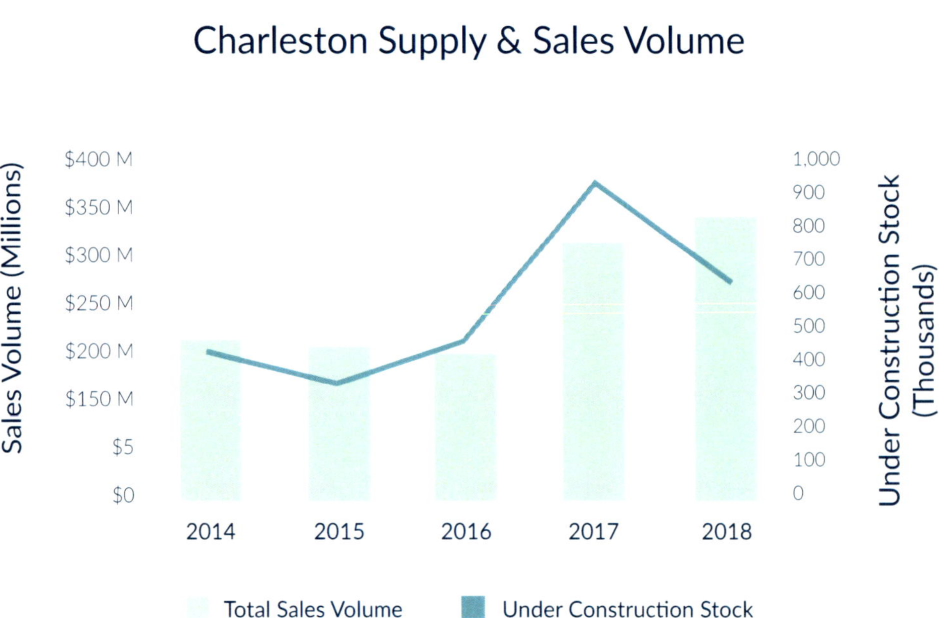

Market and economic fundamentals are extremely strong in Charleston. While tourism continues to bring a spotlight to the city. As long as manufacturing continues, from automotive companies and the Port, the city will likely remain a hotbed for investment, employment, and population growth.

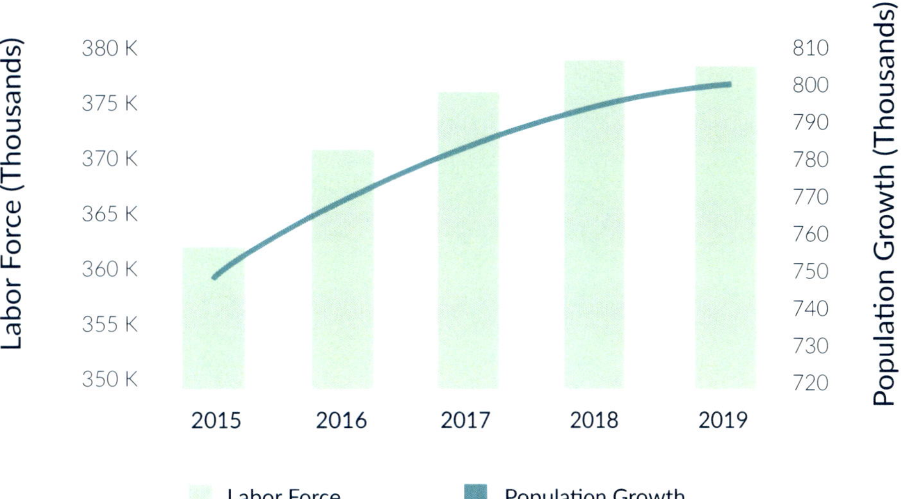

KANSAS CITY

Like Charleston, Kansas City was chosen for a surging downtown. This surge is driven by higher than average population growth, steadily growing since 2015 in large part due to a lower cost of living.

Additionally, job growth has been on the rise. Kansas City's unemployment rate is low at 3.1%, compared to the national unemployment rate of 3.6%. None other than Warren Buffet announced that GEICO selected Lenexa, a submarket of Kansas City, as its next service center. Kansas City offered an economic incentive package to the insurance company in exchange for GEICO adding 500 entry-level jobs to the economy. Incentivizing large corporations like GEICO to move into the market will continue to grow Kansas City's employment growth. This could be a strategy Kansas City continues to leverage.

Biotech research also has a massive presence in Kansas City. The healthcare IT giant, Cener Corporate, is rapidly expanding with already 900,000 sf of space in the market. After winning a $624MM contract, Cener is expected to employ more than 16,000 people over the next ten years. Additionally, Children's Research Institute is expanding their research arm and will soon employ over 3,000 researchers.

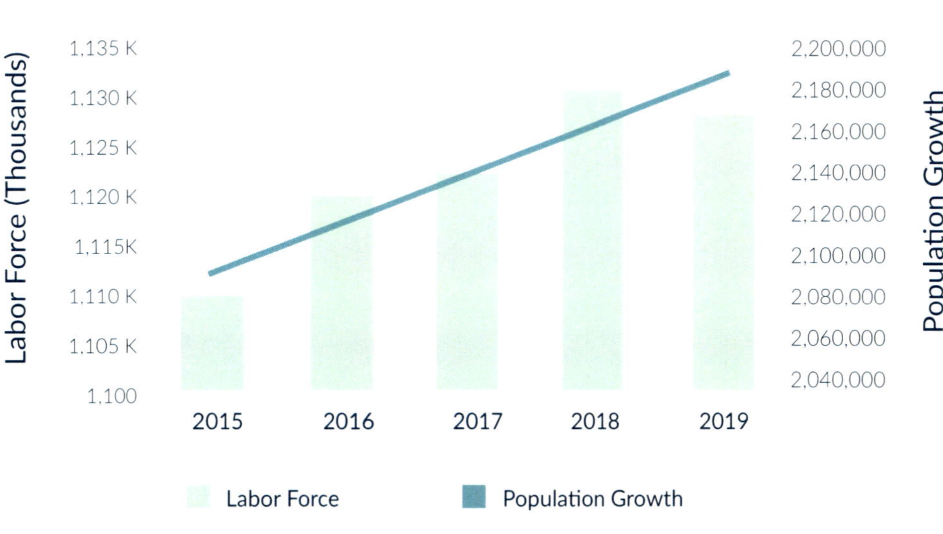

Along with biotech research, telecom companies like Sprint Corp. and AT&T occupy over 2MSF of office space and are major employers of the area. Kansas City has historically been more dependent on large employers like these but recently the city has had a spike in small business creation, an indicator of positive market health and investor confidence.

Due to Kansas City being centrally located geographically, the industrial sector has room to grow exponentially. E-commerce has revolutionized warehousing and other retailers are under pressure to have Amazon-like shipping. The need to have warehouses in centralized areas like Kansas City is crucial to national distributors and supply chain operators.

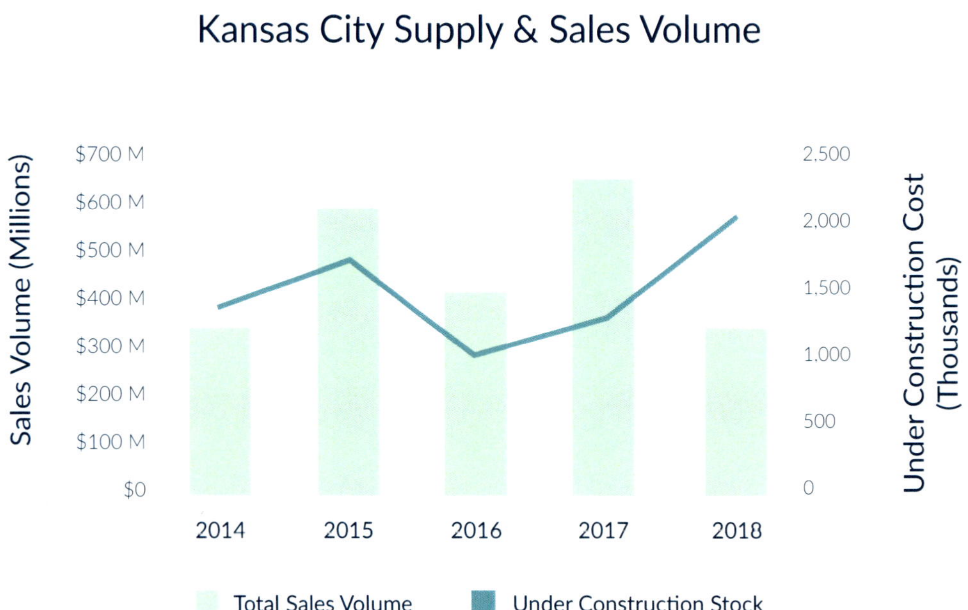

Conclusion

After reviewing our prediction from 2017, our Investment team found that Charleston proved to be the most sound case as an 18-hour city, while the other three are promising as well. Kansas City and Columbus have high job and population growth that will propel the two cities as emerging markets. Milwaukee had conflicting results, but the city is making promising strides by incentivizing companies to move into the city with tax benefits and the low cost of living and doing business.

National News & Trends

THE STATE OF THE ECONOMY

June marked ten years since the official end of the Great Recession. Broad economic indicators performed well in the second quarter of 2019 as the economy continued churning through its longest expansion period in history.

Q2 2019 REVIEW:

Economic Indicators[10]	Current	YoY Change
Consumer Price Index	255.2	+ 1.8%
Average Nonfarm Hourly Earnings	$27.83	+ 3.1%
Personal Savings Rate (% of disposable income)	6.1%	- 7.6%
Unemployment Rate	3.6%	- 5.3%
Total Employment	151.2 MM	+ 1.8%
Office Employment[11]	30.1 MM	+2.1%
Indsustrial Employment[12]	21.1 MM	+2.9%

Demographics	Current	YoY Change
Population	329.2 MM	+ 0.7%
Median Household Income (Real)	$63,976	+ 3.6%

*Source: Bureau of Labor Statistics BLS (June 2019) Unemployment Rate by State. US Average: 3.6%

- Total employment increased slightly to 151.2 million.
- Office and industrial employment had positive gains boosting by 2.1% and 2.9%, respectively. 18-hour cities generally have higher employment growth than the national average.
- Unemployment rate remains low at 3.6%, compared to the 10-year historical average of 6.6%.

[10] Consumer Price Index, Average Hourly Earnings, Personal Savings Rate (% of disposable income) and Unemployment Rate are all as of May 2019. All other economic indicators are as of 6/30/2019. Economic data source is Oxford Economics, demographic data source is Neustar and CRE data source is CoStar
[11] Office Employment are categorized by the NAICS sectors: Financial activities; Professional and business services; Information
[12] Industrial Employment are categorized by the NAICS sectors: Wholesale trade;Retail trade; Transportation and warehousing; Utilities. Manufacturing is not included)

National Office News & Trends

THE STATE OF THE OFFICE MARKET

Office Metrics	Current	YoY Change
12 Month Net Absorption[13]	70.7MSF	
Vacancy	9.6%	- 33 basis points (bps)
Supply/Under Construction	142MSF	+ 9.5%
Overall Office Gross Rent	$28.94 Full Service Gross	+ 4.7%
Total Sales Volume	$26.1B	+ 11.8%
Avg. Price Per Square Foot	$136.41	+ 11.4%
Median Cap Rate[14]	7.3%	- 11 bps
Appreciation Return[15]	0.2%	+ 70 bps
Income Return[16]	6.7%	+ 4 bps

The office market started 2019 much like it ended 2018–with slow, consistent rent growth, and minimal change to vacancy. This trend continued into the second quarter. Expect a bump in vacancy as a significant amount of office space is under construction, especially affecting key 18-hour markets like Austin, Charlotte, and Seattle. Numerous projects are under construction, and we expect many of these buildings to open without being fully leased, leading to an uptick in market vacancy rates.

This new construction is also driving up office rents, in large part due to elevated construction costs. The higher cost of raw materials and a shortage of labor are increasing the overall cost to build, so developers expect premium rents. Since the cost of raw materials is subject to increased volatility as the trade war continues, it's likely that prices will continue to push up.

[13] 12 Month Net Absorption is the change in occupied inventory for a rolling 12 month value (Source: CoStar)

[14] Median Cap rate is an unlevered initial return from the acquisition of a real estate asset calculated by dividing net operating income (NOI) by the property sales price. The cap rate is typically calculated using the NOI generated in the first year of ownership so investors can normalize and compare potential returns among competing investment properties. (Source: NAIOP)

[15] Appreciate return is the change in price value net of capital expenditures (Source: CoStar)

[16] Income Return is the portion of total return derived from income distribution. (Source: MorningStar)

Office News Headlines & Trends:

LIFE SCIENCES IS GROWING UP [17]

In 2008, the City and County of San Francisco created a special use district in Mission Bay for life science and technology companies. Currently, Mission Bay has an office vacancy rate at 0.3%, with a majority of the space occupied by tech giants who have managed to push the life sciences companies out of prime city center real estate.

With life science companies looking for a new place to call home, developers are getting creative to meet their demand for space. Opposed to the traditional life science spaces, which are akin to industrial space with high-ceiling lab space, developers are going vertical and building high rise office towers. Two buildings in South San Francisco, originally built for office use, have already been leased by life science firms and a third tower is under construction. How San Francisco and the South Bay accommodate life science firms could blaze a trail for other life science hubs such as San Diego and Boston to follow suit and build vertical.

UBER ON THE MOVE [18]

Uber Technologies, Inc. is looking to expand and has confirmed they're eyeing the up-and-coming neighborhood of Deep Ellum in the Dallas market, although a final decision timeline has not been released. The company is looking at an 8-acre, mixed-use development for a new campus location that would employ thousands of workers.

The ownership of the 8-acre development, Westdale Real Estate Investment and Management firm, recently raised $140 million by placing a portion of their real estate portfolio on the Tel Aviv Stock Exchange and could potentially use those funds to pay down the construction loan on the project.

[17] Armbrister, M. (2019, June 10). Life Science Industry Elbows Its Way Into Tight Bay Area Property Market. Retrieved from https://product.costar.com/home/news/618810624?tag=2

[18] Carlisle, C. (2019, May 20). Uber's New Destination for a Big Regional Hub Employing Thousands Could Be Dallas. Retrieved from https://product.costar.com/home/news/1738650979

The State of the National Multifamily Market

Multifamily Metrics	Current	YoY Change
12 Month Net Absorption	332.7K sf	
Vacancy	5.9%	- 9 bps
Supply/Under Construction Units	687.2K	+ 9.9%
12 Month Rent Growth	2.8%	- 20 bps
Median Price Per Unit	$112,500	+ 11.4%
Total Sales Volume	$28.3B	- 12.0%
Median Cap Rate	6.0%	+15 bps
Appreciation Return	1.5%	- 143 bps
Income Return	5.9%	- 3 bp

Strong multifamily fundamentals suggest another healthy quarter to come. Lifestyle trends such as delaying marriage and children, the desire for live-work-play communities, and high prices for single-family homes in both major and 18-hour cities are driving multifamily demand. As investors have shown an interest in Opportunity Zone development, specifically multifamily projects, construction will increase.

Multifamily News Headlines & Trends:

ZONING IN ON MULTIFAMILY [19]

Simply put, Opportunity Zones are a tax incentive for investors to reinvest capital gains in areas of economic distress. Multifamily is expected to be a key target of Opportunity Zone Funds due to the higher proportion of small to medium-sized multifamily properties that cater to low-income residents in economically underserved communities. The Federal Home Loan Mortgage Corporation (Freddie Mac) has pointed out that fewer than half of all households own their home in these zones. Freddie Mac has also reported that multifamily loan origination in Opportunity Zones has increased by 180% since the program was initiated.

[19] Heschmeyer, M. (2019, May 8). Lending Shoots Up in Opportunity Zones. Retrieved from https://product.costar.com/home/news/701094667

HIGH RISES GET BETTER WITH AGE [20]

A new demographic is taking over multifamily renting–empty nesters and retirees looking to downsize. A study done by Harvard University's Joint Center for Housing Studies shows that renters age 55 and older account for more than a quarter of all renters. These renters don't want to be tied down by ownership, nor care to keep up the maintenance of a large house when their children no longer live at home. A high rise, with a massive amount of amenities and no required up keep, is an appealing alternative.

Landlords are also rejoicing as these tenants have the money to pay top of market for a new, highly amenitized building. Additionally, many landlords feel these empty nesters and retirees are more likely to "keep up" an apartment and sign longer leases than a recent college grad. Developers are enticing this older demographic by adding larger kitchens and dining rooms, still allowing tenants to host large family gatherings, without having to maintain a large home.

The State of the National Industrial Market

Industrial Metrics	Current	YoY Change
12 Month Net Absorption	189.6 MSF	
Vacancy	4.9%	- 11 bps
Supply/Under Construction	285.3 MSF	+ 9.0%
12 Month Rent Growth	5.6%	- 80 bps
Total Sales Volume	$10.6B	- 31.2%
Average Cap Rate	6.7%	- 25 bps
Appreciation Return	4.2%	- 65 bps
Income Return	6.7%	- 2 bps

Industrial has been a favorite of investors for the past several years. Institutional owners have sought out industrial products due to the high returns and stable income often associated with the properties. Right now, the industrial market can be categorized by consistently low vacancy and high demand from investors and tenants alike. Industrial vacancy is less than half of what it was a decade ago, prior to e-commerce, which has fueled tenant demand.

[20] Owers, P. (2019, June 24). US Rental Demand Begins Rebound, Helped by Seniors. Retrieved from https://product.costar.com/home/news/417966953

Industrial News Headlines & Trends:

INDUSTRIAL ON ICE [21]

As online grocery and meal kit delivery sales rise, so does the demand for cold-storage space. Investment in temperature-controlled warehousing has climbed from $560MM in 2016 to $963MM in 2018. The industry's current foothold is 214 MSF, but according to a CBRE report,[22] the demand for cold-storage warehousing space could expand by 100 MSF by 2024, signifying growth up to 50%.

The cities most likely to experience a majority of the demand will be port cities like Los Angeles and New York, hubs that handle fresh imports from around the country and internationally. However, as cold-storage grows they will likely trickle into 18-hour markets with strong consumer demand for delivery services.

MADE IN AMERICA [23]

Amid volatile trade negotiations with China and Mexico, Stanley Black & Decker, the world's largest toolmaker, had made a push to bring manufacturing operations back to the U.S. They recently purchased a 40-acre tract in Fort Worth, TX to build a $90MM, 425,000 sf, high-tech manufacturing plant. An estimated 500 full-time employees will work at the plant with a scheduled building completion in late 2020. Trade negotiations will continue to heavily influence industrial product, especially manufacturing companies budgeting costs for raw materials, possibly inducing more companies to bring manufacturing stateside.

[21] Hirsh, L. (2019, June 12). US Cold Storage Demand Expected to Heat Up in Next Five Years. Retrieved from https://product.costar.com/home/news/1600590357?tag=4

[22] Russell, L., & Egan, D. (n.d.). Cold Storage: About to heat up? Retrieved from http://www.cbre.us/real-estate-services/real-estate-industries/industrial-and-logistics/industrial-and-logistics-research/us-marketflash---cold-storage-heating-up

[23] Carlisle, C. (2019, May 17). World's Largest Toolmaker Picks Texas to Host High-Tech Plant for Iconic Brand. Retrieved from https://product.costar.com/home/news/425131256?tag=1

The State of the National Retail Market

Retail Metrics	Current	YoY Change
12 Month Net Absorption	43.0 MSF	
Vacancy	4.5%	- 3 bps
Supply/Under Construction	71.4 MSF	- 8.0%
12 Month Rent Growth	1.4%	- 120 bps
Total Sales Volume	$11.4B	- 31.0%
Median Cap Rate	6.9%	+ 3 bps
Appreciation Return	- 1.0%	- 8 bps
Income Return	7.1%	- 3 bps

Currently, retail has the lowest vacancy rate of all property types. Interestingly, retail also has the least amount of construction (relative to overall inventory) underway. Retail's future will be exciting to watch as more retail users are repurposing nontraditional retail spaces to fit their needs, like old warehouses being turned into trendy restaurants or stores.

Retail News Headlines & Trends:

NOT YOUR SCHOOL'S FOOD HALL

A common trend in retail in recent years has been the introduction or rebranding of food halls. In a study done by Cushman & Wakefield[24], the market has quadrupled in five years. No more of the antiquated, bland, and boring dining halls like the ones from your college years. Now food halls are trendy and hip, with some of the hottest vendors in a city all centrally located.

Operators are enticing vendors with short term licenses, rather than leases, providing more flexibility as vendors prove themselves and build a local following. Many operators are implementing a single point-of-sale system to better identify outperforming or underperforming vendors. Food halls in mixed-development properties may even be the ultimate office amenity.

[24] Brown, G. (2019, May 16). FOOD HALLS 3.0: THE EVOLUTION CONTINUES (Rep.). Retrieved https://cushwake.cld.bz/Food-Halls-3-0-The-Evolution-Continues/3/#zoom=z

BREATHING LIFE & SOCIAL MEDIA INTO OUTLET CENTERS [25]

Outlet centers have a dried up pipeline. In the past two years zero discount centers have opened, nor are there any under construction. Why? Because consumers have changed the way they shop. No longer hunting in bargain stores, they are browsing the internet for deals. Outlet and discount centers are addressing this challenge by trying to entice consumers with more on-site amenities like movies, dining, and social spaces. Some centers have even designated space for social media experiences where visitors can post they were at the center in exchange for discount coupons.

The State of the National Hotel Market

Hotel Metrics[26]	Current	YoY Change
12 Month Net Absorption	60.1 K SF	
Vacancy	27.6%	- 48 bps
Supply/Stock	2.8 MSF	+ 2.4%
Net Completions 12 Mos	64.8K SF	- 9.1%
Demand[27]	$2.0MM	+ 3.1%
Rev Par Index[28]	191.7	+ 5.4%
Room Rate Index[29]	175.1	+ 3.6%

The hotel industry has enjoyed a long stretch of high levels of occupancy and growing demand. The summer months are usually the busiest for hotels. As we approach the end of summer, expect vacancy to creep up in the later months of Q3 and most of Q4. Most industry reports are projecting continuing positive growth through 2020.

[25] Hirsh, L. (2019, May 20). Outlet Centers Look for New Ways to Get Bargain Hunters off Their Couches. Retrieved from https://product.costar.com/home/news/1750344337?tag=1

[26] Please note hotel data is on a quarter lag, as of 3/31/2019. All other product type data is as of 6/30/2019.

[27] Demand is the amount of inventory occupied

[28] RevPAR Index = (Subject hotel RevPAR / Aggregated group of hotels' RevPAR) x 100

[29] Daily average room rates

Hotel News Headlines & Trends:

MY PLACE IS YOUR NEW PLACE [30]

The founder of Super 8 Hotels is betting big on his second venture, My Place. My Place offers modern hotel amenities at an affordable price for long and short stay travelers. Carving out a niche in economy hotels since 2012, My Place has expanded to 47 current locations with more locations under construction.

My Place's construction model is to build ground-up developments on one to two acre plots of land at the fringe of 18-hour cities. For example, a new My Place is coming to Avondale AZ, a suburb of the rapidly expanding Phoenix market. Being on the fringe of an emerging market enables My Place to offer lower prices to their budget customers, while benefiting from the boom of the nearby up-and-coming market.

DENVER'S SMOKING HOT(EL) MARKET [31]

Investors continue to bet on the poster child for 18-hour cities, Denver. CoStar has deemed Denver the hottest hotel city, where hotel inventory has grown by 5.1% this year, the highest ratio of new development to existing stock in any U.S. market.

The Denver market has gone through an expansion period for over a decade now. However, with the influx of construction, the market has elevated labor, material, and land costs. Coupled with low unemployment, new hotels will likely be stretched to find enough employees to staff the hotel upon completion.

[30] Drummer, R. (2019, June 17). All in the Family: Super 8 Founder Hopes to Duplicate National Success With My Place Hotels. Retrieved from https://product.costar.com/home/news/819658744?tag=2048

[31] Armbrister, M. (2019, June 4). America's Hottest Hotel City Surges on Convention Center. Retrieved from https://product.costar.com/home/news/721487584?tag=2048

SPOTLIGHTS

THE IMPACT OF THIRD PARTY LOGISTICS ON RETAIL & INDUSTRIAL

Retailers are struggling to keep up with the market pressure of two-day or same day delivery. As consumer demand mounts, retailers are looking to third party logistics for enhanced delivery efficiency which, in turn, is driving demand for warehousing space.

A 2019 Third Party Logistics (3PLs) study conducted by Infosys Consulting and Korn Ferry[32] stated that 63% of retailers are increasing their use of outsourced logistics services, a driving trend for retail and industrial. Even as e-commerce companies like Amazon dominate news headlines, they are actually dwarfed by 3PL transactions. 3PLs have been the largest occupier of warehouse space for the past two years, signing 42 MSF and accounting for nearly a third of all lease transactions.[33]

Two-day shipping has become the market standard, with same-day shipping becoming even more popular. Pushing more and more retailers to outsource shipping and handling of their products to 3PLs. 3PLs provide efficiency and expertise that retailers just don't have regarding shipping.

McKinsey[34] released a report claiming that 20-25% of the consumer market will be handled by same-day delivery service by 2025.

Thus, the demand for last mile distribution warehousing, smaller warehouses serving as the last stop between a transportation hub and the final consumer destination, is extremely high. As more last mile warehousing is built, a majority will be servicing 18-hour cities as 24-hour cities already have existing and usually efficient delivery logistics and processes.

[32] Infosys Consulting, Korn Kerry, PENSKE, & PennState. (n.d.). 2019 Third-Party Logistics Study (23rd ed., Rep.).
[33] Tolliver, J., & Salzer, C. (2019). Marketbeat U.S. Industrial Q1 2019 (Rep.). Cushman & Wakefield.
[34] Netzer, T., Krause, J., Dr., Hausmann, L., Dr., & Herrmann, N. (2014). Same-Day Delivery (Rep.). McKinsey & Company.

Because of the highly specialized nature of a fulfillment center design, the demand for build to suit warehousing has increased dramatically. A report from Cushman & Wakefield[35] stated that a third of all build-to suit-construction are logistics product. As retailers outsource their logistics, they will be able to operate more cost effectively in smaller spaces without the need of so many loading docks and warehousing space for products.

Middle Market Senior Housing Spotlight:

UNTAPPED MIDDLE MARKET

The next opportunity is in the untapped senior housing middle market as middle class baby boomers are becoming one of the largest socioeconomic groups retiring.

According to a study done by the National Investment Center (NIC),[36] the next hot opportunity in senior living–which has already hit $15.2B in investment volume–is specifically in the middle-income senior housing market. This middle market will grow by more than 6MM people within the next decade, and more than 700,000 senior housing units will be needed to serve middle-income demands.

Approximately 54% of middle-income seniors will not be able to afford assisted living that costs $60,000 annually. However, if the annual cost drops by to $50,000, an additional 2.3MM middle-income seniors could afford assisted living. This middle income demand and supply gap represents an underserved market, says NIC. To be further cost effective, middle-income seniors may select housing in 18-hour cities as an alternative to the pricier 24-hour cities.

As the Cost Of Assisted Living Decreases, the Market Expands, Presenting An Opportunity

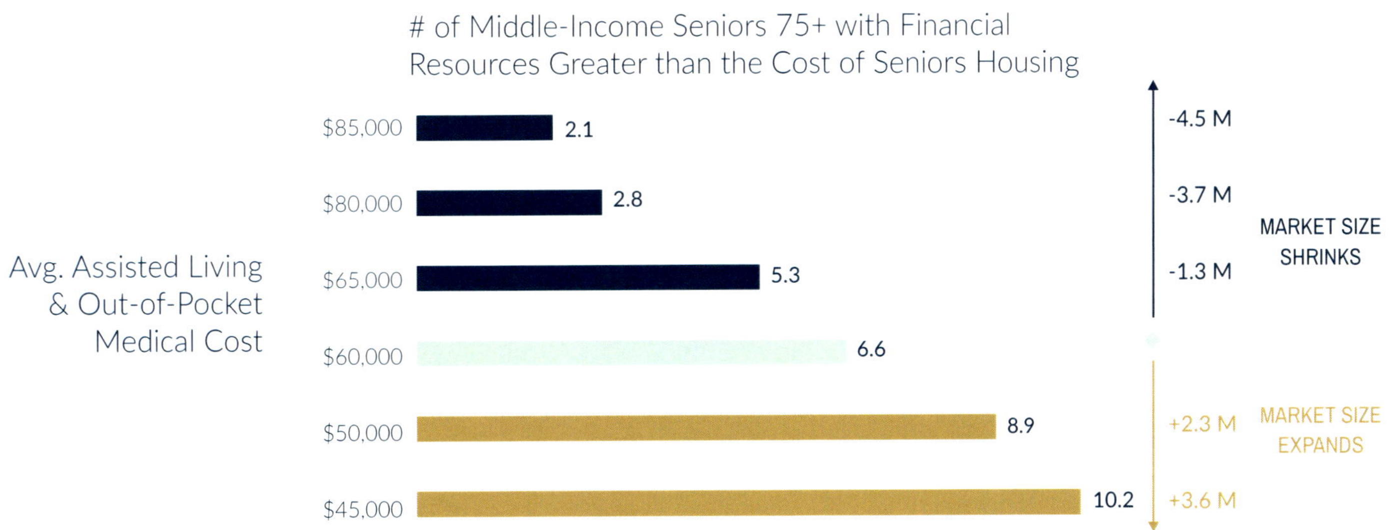

[35] Tolliver, J., & Salzer, C. (2019). Marketbeat U.S. Industrial Q1 2019 (Rep.). Cushman & Wakefield.
[36] Mace, B. B. (2019). NIC INSIDER Newsletter June 2019 (Rep.). National Investment Center.

Regional Spotlight: East Austin

LOOK AT THE CITY AND THEN STUDY THE NEIGHBORHOODS

Everyone, including us, agrees that Austin is a hot 18-hour market, but Austin is a large metro area. Each submarket comes with its own nuances, demographic trends, economic trajectory and more. So which Austin submarket do we have our eyes on? East Austin.

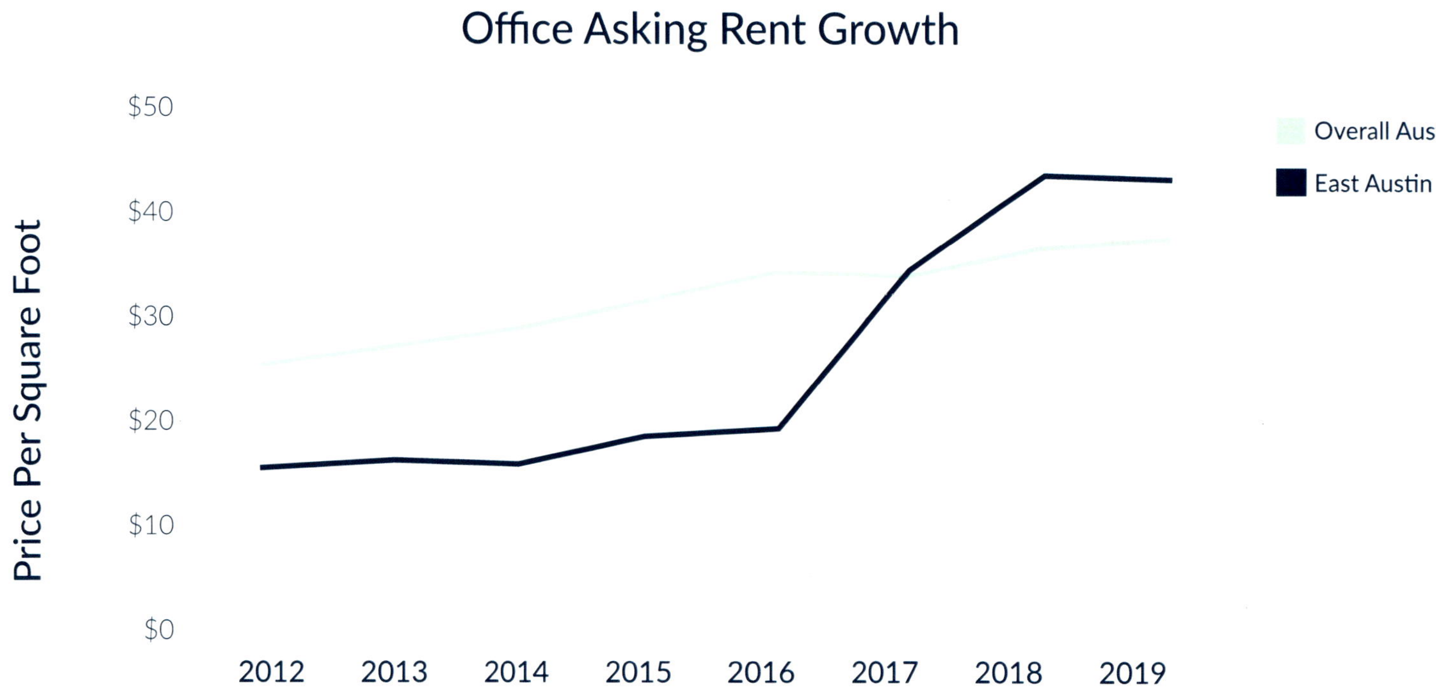

According to a CBRE report,[37] East Austin's office rates have more than doubled, growing by 162% since 2012 and out performing Austin's overall lease rates which has increased by only 43% in the same time.

Proving that Austin's tech scene is still trending, the tech sector represents 34% of leases signed in 2019. Large corporate users lease up large blocks of space, usually at the top of the market's rates, pushing lease rates higher and higher. Google just took down 150,000 sf in East Austin and the area is trying to meet the growing demand with over one MSF of office space under construction.

[37] Goebel, L., Linares, I., & Miller, E. (2019). Austin Office MarketView Q1 2019 (Rep.). CBRE.

Industry Spotlight: WeWork

CO-WORKING: DISRUPTING THE NORMS OF OFFICE SPACE

WeWork is the leader of coworking. Starting in 2010 with just one location, there are now 695 locations in 120 cities internationally. One would think that business has to be booming for such unprecedented growth... Right?

JLL's 2019 coworking report[38] stated the coworking sector has grown an average of 23% annually since 2010, which is unlike any other sector's growth. In 2018 alone, coworking accounted for approximately two-thirds of the national office market occupancy gains.

Some landlords are relieved to have WeWork lease up 40,000-120,000 sf of their building. But other landlords can only lease to creditworthy tenants, and WeWork is not a creditworthy tenant.

[38] JLL Research. (2019). Flexible space evolves (Rep.). JLL.

Furthermore, leasing to WeWork can come with high tenant improvement allowances and invasive build outs, making them an unattractive tenant. Their redemption comes in the lease terms–usually signing longer term leases at top of market prices. When signing leases, WeWork signs under an LLC, after putting down a significant security deposit to render the cost of the build out. But they only guarantee a portion of their lease term length, leaving the balance of the term to be held liable by the limited liability company. This relieves WeWork of liability for the full length of the lease.

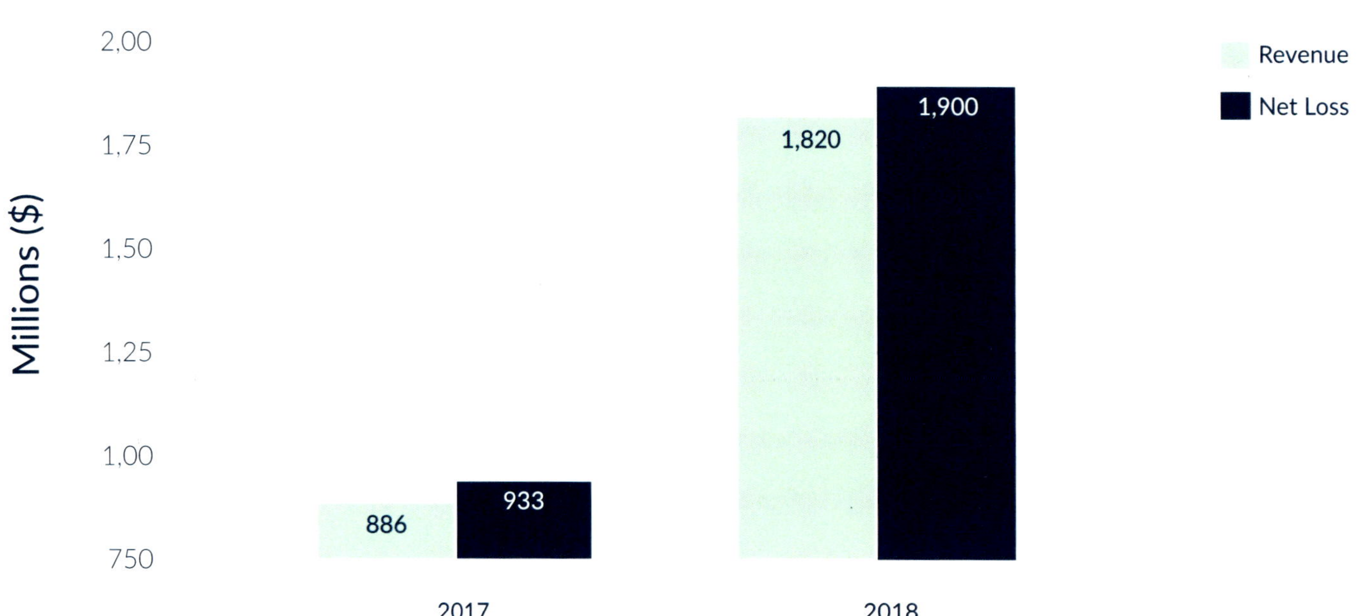

Even though WeWork has made significant jumps in revenue from 2017 to 2018, so has their net loss. Their net margin is negative and overall growth is flat. As WeWork approaches a possible IPO, analysts are scrutinizing WeWork's profitability despite revenue growing by 105.4% in one year.[39]

CrowdStreet's VP of Investments, Ian Formigle believes, "the fatal blow for WeWork may be the IPO itself. In a market downturn, you can easily see a scenario where, on the heels of successive disappointing quarterly results, the street decimates its stock price. In that event, what follows is a downward spiral of rising debt costs and bad press that accelerates beyond the company's control. Faced with such a prospect, the prudent move is for WeWork is to stay private until the next cycle emerges."

Further, Formigle predicts "WeWork is headed for a major correction in the next downturn. With losses that have been doubling year-over-year (and losses that exceed total revenues), a decrease in office leasing demand is all that is needed for the company to experience a full-blown crisis. The type of tenant to whom WeWork caters has the most elastic demand for office space. Many of its current tenants like WeWork mainly for the camaraderie and cool vibe and not for getting actual work done, which makes WeWork's space a "nice to have" but not "must have". In a downturn, the people coming out of the basement to take space at WeWork can easily go back to the basement."

[39] Sourced from WeWork Financials

CONCLUSION

We believe that 18-hour cities with strong population and employment growth, coupled with a relatively low cost of doing business, provide investors with the best range of commercial real estate investing opportunities.

KEY TAKEAWAYS FROM OUR ANALYSIS:

- We believe the most promising emerging 18-hour city is Charleston, SC.
- In order to keep up with consumer demand for two-day shipping, retailers are outsourcing shipping and handling to third party logistics (3PLs). Those 3PLs are fueling demand for warehouse space.
- The senior housing middle market demands are not being met by current inventory, providing the opportunity to reach an underserved (and growing) market.
- WeWork, and coworking in general, have grown tremendously. However, WeWork's net losses outweigh revenue. Despite our overall optimism about co-working as an office space solution, we having growing skepticism about WeWork's business model as a possible IPO approaches.

Commercial real estate is not a monolith. While what is happening on the national scale inevitably has a local impact, the unique factors of a regional market have an even greater impact on a project's long-term success. Where people and their money is moving to, how much confidence there is in the local economy, and what kind of demand there is for a specific asset type in an area are all factors that investors need to weigh when evaluating an investment opportunity.

The Comprehensive Guide to Commercial Real Estate Investing

Everything you need to know to succeed in the new world of open-access, online commercial real estate investing.

WITH IAN FORMIGLE
VP Investments, CrowdStreet

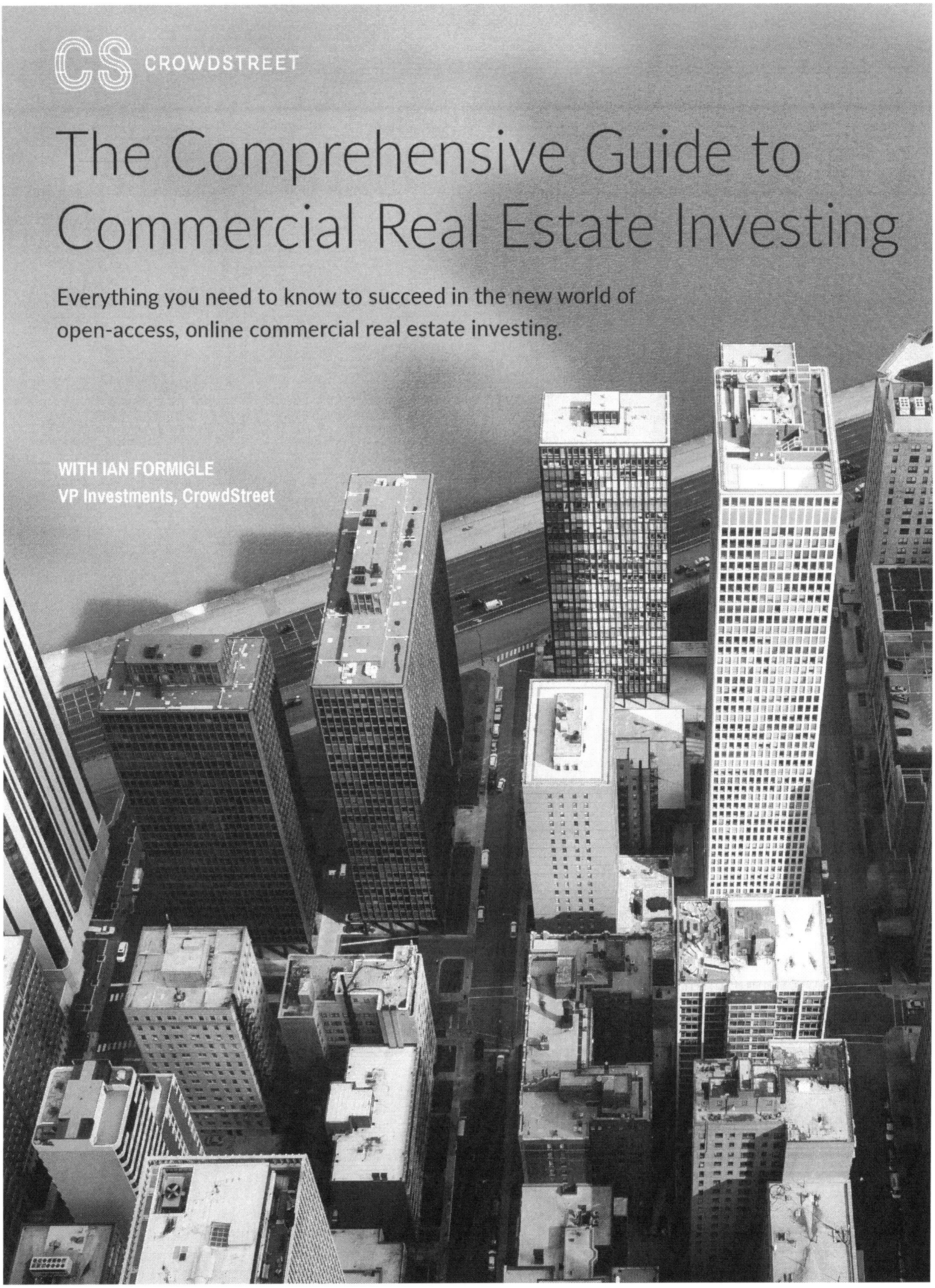

Table of Contents

UNDERSTANDING RISK & REWARD

DIVERSIFICATION & REAL ESTATE

The commercial real estate investing renaissance period has begun.

This analogy may seem far fetched to you, but it's true. Just a few years ago, we were still languishing in the dark ages of commercial real estate investing.

It was a primitive and closed off world that was dominated by a select few who enjoyed privileged access to deal flow and capital. Information was spread by word of mouth and investor access was granted only to "members of the court". The system was structured to preserve the concentration of power and reward the elite at the expense of the masses.

Today, we are in the early phase of a renaissance period for commercial real estate investing and the catalyst is real estate crowdfunding. Through new legislation and advancements in technology, information and access to opportunity is now widely disseminated. While still in its infancy, access to direct real estate investment opportunities is broadening to include everyday individual investors throughout the U.S. who, until recently, were shut out of the conversation. This broadening of access is disrupting the traditional flow of capital and is threatening to topple the current regime.

Welcome to our guide. I'm Ian Formigle and together you'll learn everything you need to know about CRE Investing.

The commercial real estate investing renaissance period has begun, bringing with it an age of enlightenment. Intellectual movements are great, provided that the new access to information is worthwhile and relevant to you. This begs the question, "should I be investing in commercial real estate? And if so, why?"

The answer is a resounding "yes!" and the fundamental reason why is that direct investments into commercial real estate should comprise a portion of every investor's portfolio. At a total market cap estimated at upwards of $15 trillion in the U.S. alone, commercial real estate is the third largest asset class behind equities and bonds.

So, if commercial real estate is the third largest asset class, then why isn't it already a pervasive part of investors' portfolios? Part of the answer dates back to the 1930's when passage of the Securities Act of 1933 made it difficult for smaller investors to access private securities, which commercial real estate largely comprises. This depression era change in legislation induced a trend towards consolidation of capital into fewer and fewer hands. The result of this trend is that, today, much of that $15 trillion of commercial real estate stock is controlled by relatively few players.

The existing environment in commercial real estate is why the passage of the Jumpstart Our Business Startups Act ("JOBS") act of 2012 was a landmark event for the industry. We'll delve into greater detail of why later but, essentially, when Title II of this act was enacted in September of 2013, it began to break down the walls that had been keeping control of commercial real estate concentrated amongst fewer investors.

Post JOBS Act, the veiled secrecy that the Securities Act of 1933 mandated has been lifted. With diminished ability to leverage secrecy to their advantage, the larger players are beginning to lose control of the information flow. Conversely, enhanced information flow is now enabling smaller investors to become aware of investment opportunities and to begin to understand them. As smaller investors begin to understand these investment opportunities, larger numbers of them can assemble to invest.

Understanding commercial real estate investing is the point of this book. Understanding commercial real estate is worthwhile because access to commercial real estate investing is improving by the day. That increased access is now creating a virtuous cycle of investors wanting to discover investment opportunities all over the U.S., not just in their backyard. At the same time, commercial real estate sponsors are interested in growing their investor bases to expand across the U.S., not just their backyard.

When rapidly growing numbers of two sides of a series of transactions seek to discover each other, you have the foundation of a successful marketplace. This phenomenon, which is transpiring right now in the commercial real estate industry, is precisely what the CrowdStreet Marketplace leverages - the desire of investors and sponsors desire to discover each other through a scalable online solution.

A PERSONAL JOURNEY

My personal journey into the world of online real estate crowdfunding investing dates back to the summer of 2013.

At the time, I was an acquisitions officer for a commercial real estate private equity group and focused on my next deal. My firm was known within the industry as an "Operator" meaning that we sought to acquire, operate and ultimately sell commercial real estate assets for a profit. We funded our portfolio assets with three primary sources of equity: 1) large institutional investors - the types of groups that manage pension fund money 2) high net worth individual investors that were "friends and family" of our firm and 3) our firm's balance sheet capital.

Late that summer, my firm was approached by an entrepreneur named Darren Powderly. Darren had been studying the recently passed JOBS Act and was focusing on Title II of the Act, which when implemented later that year, would enable for the first time since 1933, general solicitation, or advertising of private investment offerings. Darren explained that once private offerings could be publicly advertised they could be put online. Commercial real estate was arguably best poised to harness this broad reach since it was such a vast and tangible asset class. He envisioned a new world of online finance where people could invest in commercial real estate anywhere in the world effortlessly from their laptops. To address this upcoming opportunity, he started a company called CrowdStreet.

That first meeting left a deep impression on me. Following that meeting, my boss, the co-founder and CEO of the firm, told me that he had a strong feeling that this was the next big thing in our industry and that we should formulate a plan to get ahead of the curve. He and I agreed that what Darren had just outlined could be a game changer.

Title II of the JOBS Act was enacted in September of 2013, but it was during Q1 of 2014 that the space began to take off. A flurry of press and national interest provided the catalyst for our firm to accelerate our analysis of the space. I was tapped as the person to figure it out so, over the ensuing six months, I studied real estate crowdfunding intensely, speaking with CEO's of these new online platforms, analyzing the new legislation and interviewing attorneys at the forefront of the movement.

Through my analysis, I became convinced of the following:

1. The online movement that was underway was the tip of the iceberg - online real estate investing would only gain more momentum over time.
2. As it gained momentum, it had the potential to disrupt traditional real estate capital markets.
3. The most interesting and transformative part of this movement was the adoption of technology in an industry that had historically shunned it.

At the conclusion of my analysis, I identified two platforms to partner with to launch deals, one of which was CrowdStreet. In the summer of 2014, during a meeting over coffee, Darren and his co-founder partner, Tore Steen, broached the subject of their plans for growth. Their first two deals on the platform were well-received, which had helped enable them to attract two venture capital firms to lead the funding of their seed round. With the prospect of a seed round looking good, CrowdStreet was now poised to identify the next principal to become its version of a Chief Investment Officer.

Despite the fact that my current position afforded me great opportunity within the real estate private equity world, I was already sold on the promising future of commercial real estate crowdfunding. CrowdStreet presented an opportunity for me to help change an industry.

And so that is the story of how I became Vice President of Investments at CrowdStreet.

The vision of 2013 is now a reality. Commercial real estate crowdfunding is a generational opportunity for individual investors to access the types of investments previously reserved for institutions. However, investing like an institution requires knowledge. This book will break it down and teach you how it works.

WHAT TO EXPECT

In this book, we'll begin by discussing why commercial real estate should comprise a part of every investor's portfolio. We'll move on from there to delve into why I have found that real estate crowdfunding provides a superior vehicle for individual investors to gain exposure to direct real estate investments.

From here, we'll dig into the meat of the text where I walk you through each asset class and how to successfully invest in them. We'll then move on to breaking down the key metrics and industry tricks of the trade that commercial real estate professionals use to evaluate deals.

Once we have covered asset classes and commercial real estate metrics, you'll be ready to use that knowledge to begin evaluating risk and identifying opportunities for reward. We'll even walk through hypothetical deals to compare and evaluate relative risk and understand volatility of targeted returns. This portion of the book is where the rubber hits the road.

In the final chapters of this book, we pull it all together to apply the knowledge gained to the concepts of building a diversified real estate investment portfolio.

The bottom line is that it's time for investors to begin understanding, accessing and investing in commercial real estate, an asset class that, in the years ahead, should be as critical to an investor's portfolio as stocks and bonds are today.

I can help you solve the challenges of understanding and accessing commercial real estate investments.
The investing part is up to you.

With that, let's dive in!

Why Commercial Real Estate Investing?

Top 6 Reasons to Invest in Commercial Real Estate

U.S. commercial real estate sales topped $435 billion in 2015, according to JLL. The near record volume of private and institutional capital flowing into the U.S. commercial and multifamily real estate market is a testament to the appeal of the asset class. Here are six reasons why commercial real estate is attracting a broader investor audience to the sector.

Investors don't have to look much further than the recent volatility on Wall Street to understand why real estate investment is in vogue. However, commercial real estate has a long history of being an attractive investment play during both up and down market cycles.

The near record volume of private and institutional capital flowing into the U.S. commercial and multifamily real estate market is a testament to the appeal of the asset class. U.S. commercial real estate sales topped $435 billion in 2015, according to JLL. Both domestic and international investors are looking to the U.S. as a safe haven to place capital as a strategy to both preserve their original investment and generate a positive return.

There are a number of current micro- and macro-level dynamics fueling that strong investor appetite for real estate. Chief among them is concerns about slowing growth in China and the negative impact that might have on the global economy. Direct real estate investment also offers a number of benefits, including, but not limited to, stability, portfolio diversity, cash flow and appreciation. Below is a closer look at some of the top reasons that commercial real estate is attracting a broader investor audience to the sector.

1 **Attractive returns:** One of the main reasons that institutional and private investors alike are pursuing real estate investments right now is that they are chasing yields. Real estate returns are attractive compared to alternatives in stocks, bonds or even other commodities such as gold. One benchmark for measuring investment performance for a large pool of individual commercial real estate properties in the private market is the National Council of Real Estate Investment Fiduciaries (NCREIF) Property Index, which measures the performance of an immense pool of individual commercial real estate properties on an unleveraged basis. The NCREIF Index reported an annual return of 12.7% in 2015, which bested other key indexes such as the S&P 500, Dow 30 and Russell 2000. On a longer term view, the NCREIF Index has reported an average annual return of 8.8% over the past 15 years, which is 200 basis points above the average performance of the S&P 500 for the same period.

2 **Cash flow:** Real estate investments are often structured to deliver steady cash flow with dividends that are distributed to investors monthly, quarterly or annually. The two main options for investors are to make either an equity investment or a debt investment.

Equity investments on the CrowdStreet Marketplace involve buying a passive, minority ownership stake in a hard asset, such as an apartment community or office building. High occupancies and rising rents generally deliver what most owners/investors strive for – steady or rising cash flow over time.

Debt investments refer to investing in a real estate loan. Those loans are backed by an underlying asset as collateral, such as land or a building. One of the advantages of debt investments is that they are generally structured to deliver a fixed return. For example, in 2014 the CrowdStreet Marketplace offered a $6 million mezzanine (second position) loan investment on behalf of Everwest Real Estate Partners ("Everwest"). Everwest offered CrowdStreet investors a 10.5% fixed interest rate paid quarterly over a targeted five-year term. The collateral is a 687,000 SF, 91% leased, four-building business park located in the New York Metro area with AT&T as the anchor tenant. In this case, Everwest is the lender so CrowdStreet investors are benefitting from the opportunity to co-invest alongside the loan manager in a loan that was already closed and paying a current return.

3 **Equity upside:** Specific to equity investments, investors have the opportunity to boost their overall return by cashing in on property appreciation or a capital gain on an asset once it is sold. Property values certainly rise and fall during market cycles, which makes timing the exit strategy a critical aspect of maximizing investor value. Some investors can reap the rewards of opportunistic buys that allow them to buy, fix and flip an asset in a relatively short period, such as one to three years. Other investment strategies, more predicated on the prospect of stable cash flows, might target a hold period of five to seven years or longer.

4 **Depreciation:** While realizing appreciation and capital gains is a definite incentive to real estate ownership, there also is depreciation on the other end of the spectrum. Depreciation decreases the accounting value of the physical structure of a real estate asset, as most assets decline in value over time, but does not affect the market value of a property. In its most basic form, the physical improvements of a property may be depreciated over a 27.5 year period in an accounting method referred to as "straight line depreciation". However, certain improvements (e.g. appliances and flooring) may be depreciated over a period as short as five years. Depreciation is utilized by real estate operators as a tax benefit tool, which allows an investor to utilize a passive "loss" from depreciating improvements to offset other passive income. The net result is a higher after-tax yield. As the tax benefits of depreciation are dependent upon an individual's or entity's taxable income, investors are strongly encouraged to consult a tax advisor.

> "Commercial real estate offers a number of unique attributes as an investment. Here we cover six of them."

5 **Principal Paydown:** For assets that are mortgaged with a fully amortizing loan (in most cases over a 30-year period), the property's revenues service an outstanding debt that reduces with each month's payment. Think of it as a monthly savings program - the rents paid by a property's tenants reduce the asset's leverage, which in turn, increases equity and, hence, investor returns at the point of exit (which at 75% leverage can amount to 25% of total returns) while also reducing risk. In a world of investment uncertainty, principal paydown infuses an element of month-over-month certainty of returns.

6 **Tangible assets:** Another key advantage of real estate investing is that it is a good way to diversify portfolios that are backed by hard assets. Real estate is not the same as buying shares in a company that may be here today and gone tomorrow. Certainly, cases such as Enron and Lehman Brothers have proved that even stalwart corporations are not infallible. Real estate is an asset class that investors can literally touch and feel. Yes, some building occupants

may come and go, and there may be ups and downs in building valuations over the course of its life, but the property itself is not going to disappear.

As we've highlighted above, there are many great reasons to invest in commercial real estate. Unfortunately, CRE investment opportunities have historically been limited to minimum $250,000 investments - putting the class out of reach to all but the most deep pocketed investors.

However, legislation, including the 2012 JOBS act, has recently helped launched a new class of online real estate marketplaces that is democratizing access to commercial real estate deal flow. Platforms such as the CrowdStreet Marketplace now make direct commercial real estate easily accessible to accredited investors. The platform gives investors transparent information on a variety of commercial real estate investment opportunities across the country, as well as providing tools to help investors track performance and manage their own growing real estate investment portfolios.

CrowdStreet is unique in that it only lists institutional-quality commercial real estate investment opportunities and never charges fees for investors to join or invest.

Making the Jump From Single-Family to Commercial Real Estate Investing

The first step into real estate investing for individuals often involves investing in the asset class that they best understand – single-family residences ("SFR"). However investing in SFR often presents a number of challenges including limited cash flow, no economies of scale, binary occupancy and more. For these reason and many more, once investors are ready to begin thinking about real estate investing as part of a diversified portfolio, the logical move is to transition to commercial real estate investing. In this chapter we illustrate the multiple advantages CRE provides over SFR, and provide the foundational knowledge necessary for you to make the jump to commercial real estate investing.

The first step into real estate investing for individuals often involves investing in the asset class that they best understand – single-family residences ("SFR"). It's logical for investors to start here since they have typically already been through the experience of purchasing a SFR. In addition to experience, understanding value is relatively easy as there is a lot of free online information readily available (e.g. Zillow) on the SFR the market. However, some of the challenges of investing in SFR's are as follows:

1. There is typically little cash flow (unless you are acquiring unleveraged)
2. Unforeseen capital expenditures can wipe out years of cash flow and tank returns
3. There are no economies of scale at the asset level
4. It is extremely hands on
5. Occupancy is binary (100% or 0%); and
6. Most of your competition is not seeking to acquire an investment but a place to call home, which can remove objectivity from the bidding process

Therefore, once investors are ready to begin thinking about real estate investing as part of a diversified portfolio, the logical move is to transition to commercial real estate investing.

Commercial real estate is an increasingly popular alternative asset class. It is also the third largest asset class after equities and bonds. The commercial real estate market is gigantic and can require rigorous analysis and predetermined investing strategies. Yet spending the time to get up to speed on this asset class can be well worth the effort. As we noted in our chapter, "Invest like Harvard: The Advantages of Direct Real Estate Investing" some of the world's most sophisticated investors invest heavily into commercial real estate and are handsomely rewarded. In recent years, commercial real estate has been the strongest performing component of diversified portfolios.

The good news is that there are similarities that carry over from SFR into the commercial real estate investing. Numerous terms and metrics such as debt, equity, loan to value, occupancy, net operating income, cash on cash returns, and dozens more apply to all forms of real estate, regardless of the product type. Yet there also are distinct differences between SFR and commercial real estate both in terms of each asset class's merits as well as how deals are structured.

Equity deals offer greater upside

When looking at the structure under which SFR investing is conducted on most online investment platforms, it is important to understand that most residential investments listed offer a debt financing investment on a "fix-and-flip" strategy and not a traditional buy and hold strategy. In most cases, the online offering is for a short-term, fixed-rate loan, such as a 10-month bridge loan at a high single-digit interest rate.

Commercial real estate offers debt and equity investment opportunities. Debt investors provide leverage at a fixed rate for someone else to own property but with a lien on the asset as collateral for the loan. Equity investors acquire an interest in the property. Equity investors share in the upside when a property meets or exceeds expectations in operating income and they also receive their pro rata share of value appreciation at the time of a property sale. To learn more about debt investing, please check out our chapter on "Real Estate Debt Fund Investing 101".

Building Portfolio Diversification

> "Investing in single family homes is a fine way to get started in real estate investing but it lacks most of the benefits of an institutional-quality investment. In this section, I discuss why serious investors look to commercial real estate."

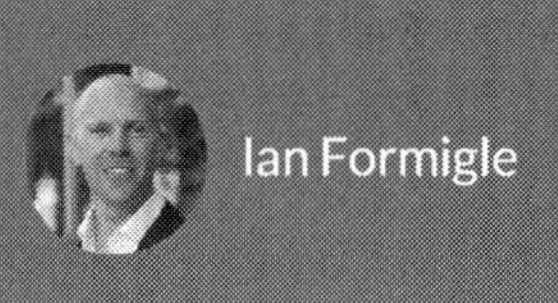

It is true that the SFR market has attracted interest from institutional investors in recent years. However, this interest was predicated on a macro opportunity in SFR's that was attributable to the housing crash. Now that this once in a generation type opportunity is gone, many institutional players are actually now looking to realize profits and liquidate portfolios. The current SFR market is now largely back to being more micro-market in nature.

Commercial real estate is a substantially larger and more diverse market. For example, investment sales for commercial and multifamily properties valued greater than $5 million topped $540 billion last year alone. The stock and variety of commercial real estate is vast in comparison to SFR. With each asset class possessing its own drivers and cycles, it also creates opportunities to invest in commercial real estate for a variety of reasons and at different times. If you invest in SFR, you are always buying into (or selling into) the same macro story no matter where you invest.

There are many different points that investors can enter the commercial market for both debt and equity deals. For example, investors can place capital into institutional-quality apartments, hotels, office buildings, shopping centers and industrial facilities. Investors have more choices to select investments they are comfortable with, and, as mentioned above, it also makes it easier to build diversity into portfolios as investors continue to grow their real estate holdings. For more information on commercial real estate portfolio diversification please see our chapter titled, "How to Build a Diversified Real Estate Portfolio Using Crowdfunded Real Estate"

Grounded in economics

Another consideration when comparing SFR to commercial real estate is the rationality of the market. Single-family homes that rely on a fix-and-flip model cater to the whims of today's homebuyers. Homeownership is at its lowest level in nearly 50 years. In addition, approaching the SFR market with an analytical investor approach can be challenging as homebuyers can be fickle. A variety of wild cards can pop up to kill a sale and delay an exit strategy that can range from a bad choice in paint color to a neighbor that doesn't do yard work. SFR prices can also be highly sensitive (far more than multifamily) to municipal decision making such as school district remapping.

In contrast, commercial real estate is more fundamentally tied to logical demand drivers. Businesses location decisions are based on facts, such as proximity to customers and workers. Retail assets depend upon daily traffic counts along its frontage, something that is easily searchable. Industrial assets require certain clear heights (e.g. 24' or 36'), dock high or ground level loading and proximity to major roadways. That rational context makes it easier for investors to understand, analyze and draw conclusions about investment opportunities.

While more rational, commercial real estate investments can arguably be more complex. So, it is important for investors to do their due diligence and peel back the layers to look at how a deal is structured. That information is typically transparent and readily available in offering documents, but it is important to know where to look and interpret its meaning. To that point, some of the terms and resources that are unique to commercial real estate include:

1. Sponsor promote fee structures
2. Preferred returns
3. Sources & uses
4. Core, Core-plus, Value-added and Opportunistic investing strategies
5. The capital stack

Single-family residential is a good place to start real estate investing, because it does hit the "comfort zone" for many investors. It is a product type and business model that people are familiar with and it is relatively easy to understand. But for investors that are looking to tap into the true power of real estate investing and invest like the best and the brightest institutional investment managers, that means stepping up to commercial real estate assets.

Given the scale and complexities of commercial real estate investing, a great way for investors to get exposure to the asset class is to invest passively with proven operators who utilize their expertise to earn consistent returns in a more sophisticated but rational market.

Why Real Estate?

The Changing Dynamics of Real Estate Crowdfunding

The sector is shaking off its ill-fitting "crowdfunding" label and gaining recognition for simply what it is – online real estate investing.

Real estate crowdfunding has experienced explosive growth and transformative change since its debut in late 2013. One of the most notable shifts is that the sector is shaking off its ill-fitting "crowdfunding" label and gaining recognition for simply what it is – online real estate investing.

To its credit, crowdfunding has unlocked the financial power of the crowd. Masses of people around the U.S., and around the world, are now investing in a wide variety of business start-ups, new ideas and innovative technologies via online platforms. There is no doubt that crowdfunding is flexing some financial muscle, with global capital raising capabilities forecasted to reach $34.4 billion in 2015, according to Massolution, a Los Angeles-based research and advisory firm.

The same legislation that opened the doors to crowdfunding has also helped launch the rise of online real estate investment marketplaces. The Jumpstart Our Business Startups, or JOBS Act, that was passed in 2012 removed a key obstacle by allowing private real estate offerings to be directly advertised to accredited investors.

Since September of 2013, platforms such as CrowdStreet have been able to present institutional-quality real estate offerings backed by best-in-class sponsors and a solid business plan designed to deliver an attractive return to investors. Case in point, CrowdStreet's first Marketplace offering, Mainstreet - Bloomington, which was realized in August of 2015, delivered a 10% annualized current yield to investors, paid quarterly, with an additional 4% annualized accrued return paid at redemption; a return exactly in line with Mainstreet's original pro forma.

While the JOBS Act paved the way for the creation of online real estate investing marketplaces, there is nothing new about private real estate offerings. Commercial real estate is an established industry that has been relying on private investment capital for centuries. U.S. commercial real estate investment sales alone topped $435 billion last year while billions more went to new construction, renovation and redevelopment projects. Online real estate investing is a small, but rapidly growing part of the broader commercial real estate capital markets - one that is expected to play a significantly larger role in the future.

> "Changing legislation and advances in technology have made online commercial real estate investing (with sub $20k minimums) a reality. It's a trend that is only gaining momentum."
>
> 
> Ian Formigle

Driving this shift is the fact that the fundraising activities, which real estate sponsors and syndicators used to execute offline, are rapidly transitioning online. A combination of legislative changes and new technology platforms such as the Crowd-Street Marketplace are enabling accredited investors to invest online in real estate in much the same way as they buy stocks and bonds from an online brokerage account. The days when real estate operators had to rely on raising investment capital at the golf course or over drinks at the country club are slipping into the past. For investors, the end result is that private real estate investing opportunities, that have traditionally been highly exclusive, are now more widely accessible to individuals.

Technology is also transforming private real estate investing by bringing greater efficiency and transparency to the process. The CrowdStreet Marketplace gives accredited investors access to online investing tools that allow them to view offer information, complete offer transactions, receive post-funding updates and track investment performance. Investors aren't the only stakeholders to benefit - sponsors are seeing transformative gains from these tools as well. In addition to the Marketplace, CrowdStreet also offers a private label software-as-a-service (SaaS) solution with its Sponsor Direct portal that allows sponsors to offer online real estate fundraising and investor management capabilities on their own branded websites, allowing sponsors to provide the same streamlined online investor acquisition and management solutions directly to their own existing investors.

CrowdStreet has created a powerful online solution for what has traditionally been a brick-and-mortar business model. Just as Amazon and other online firms are revolutionizing the retail industry, CrowdStreet is transforming the commercial real estate playing field by drastically simplifying the online funding process for direct real estate investment.

Invest like Harvard: How to Profit from Direct Real Estate Investing

For fiscal year 2015 Harvard's direct real estate investments posted the highest annual return of all portfolio asset classes at 35.5%, trouncing U.S. equity and private equity holdings, which returned 12.4% and 11.8% respectively. In this chapter we outline Harvard's direct investment real estate strategy and show how you can access similar direct investment opportunities through existing online investment marketplaces.

There are plenty of pundits who offer advice on how to "invest like the pros". However, investors who are looking to enhance the performance of their investment portfolios probably won't find a better investment model than the one used by the $37.6 billion endowment for Harvard University.

The entity in charge of managing the endowment, Harvard Management Company (HMC), has accrued an impressive investment track record across its 41-year history. As of fiscal year 2015, the endowment had produced an average annual return of 12.2% – 290 basis points higher than the average 9.3% return of a typical U.S. 60/40 stock and bond portfolio.

The methodology behind HMC's success is the application of what is known as Modern Portfolio Theory. Modern Portfolio Theory is a theory of finance that seeks to maximize portfolio returns by carefully allocating capital across multiple asset classes.

Among those asset classes, Modern Portfolio Theory calls for 10% to 20% of a well-diversified portfolio to be allocated into hard real estate assets. Historical results show that strategy to be effective in posting above-market returns in both good and poor market conditions.

> "Harvard has a 41-year track record of trouncing the performance of a typical stock and bond portfolio. How did they do it? By investing in commercial real estate."
>
> 
> Ian Formigle

For example, fiscal 2015 was a challenging year for many investors as global markets reacted to falling oil prices and concerns of slowing growth in China. However, Harvard's annual return of 5.8% outperformed a number of other benchmark indexes, and real estate played a leading role in boosting the endowment's overall return for the year. Specifically, Harvard's direct real estate investments posted the highest annual return of all portfolio asset classes at 19.4%, trouncing its second and third best performing asset classes, U.S. equity and private equity holdings, which returned 12.4% and 11.8% respectively.

According to a letter from HMC President Stephen Blyth, Ph.D., in the endowment's 2015 fiscal report, the real estate return of 19.4% was driven primarily by the "exceptional, continued success of a direct investment strategy started in 2010." In fiscal year 2015, the Harvard direct real estate program returned 35.5%, as our internal real estate team and their joint venture partners continued to create outstanding value throughout their portfolio," stated Blyth. That performance reinforces the advantages that can be found by devoting a percentage of an investment portfolio to real estate assets. It also emphasizes the important distinction that exists between direct real estate investing versus other real estate investment options such as buying shares of publicly traded REIT stocks.

Asset allocation is the most fundamental strategic investment decision an investor can make, and even Blyth admits that it can be the most challenging. Those strategic asset allocation targets vary from investor to investor. HMC recently took a fresh look at its own strategy, and after considerable research and market analysis, the company reconfirmed its commitment to real estate in 2016 with a target range of 10% to 17%.

Most accredited investors don't have the deep bench of investment resources as a major institutional entity such as Harvard. However, investors do have greater access to direct real estate investment opportunities than ever before via the online real estate marketplace. Platforms such as the CrowdStreet Marketplace now make direct commercial real estate easily accessible to accredited investors. The platform gives investors transparent information on a variety of commercial real estate investment opportunities across the country, as well as providing tools to help investors track performance and manage their own growing real estate investment portfolios.

10 Reasons to Invest with Real Estate Crowdfunding

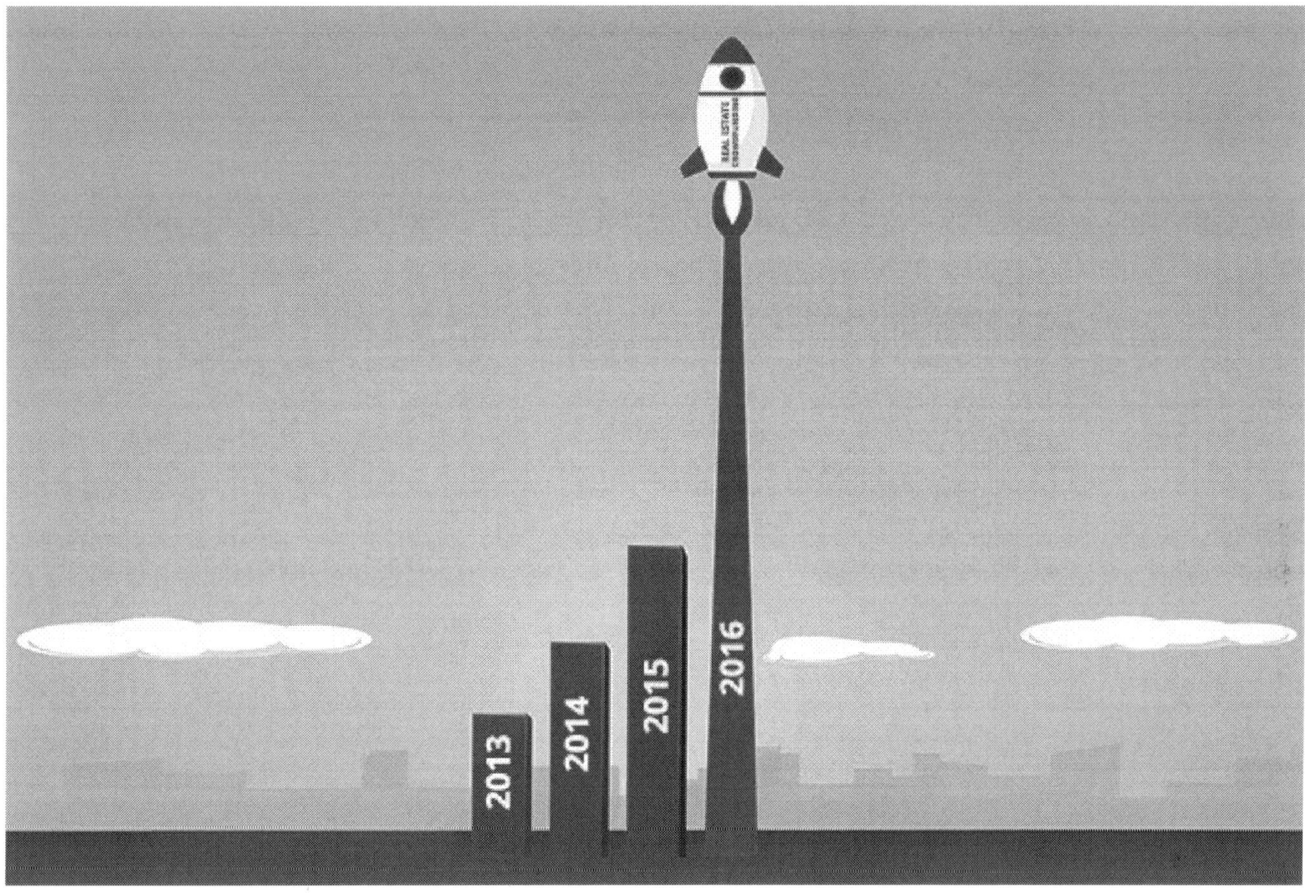

Real estate crowdfunding is experiencing explosive growth as investors witness its maturation into an increasingly mainstream form of online direct real estate investing. In this chapter, we discuss the top ten reasons investors are adopting real estate crowdfunding and provide details on how to get started with as little as $10,000.

The explosive growth occurring in the real estate crowdfunding industry validates why investors are being increasingly drawn to the space. Title II of the Jumpstart our Business Startups or "JOBS" Act, passed in September of 2013, provided the catalyst for the emergence of online marketplaces dedicated to direct real estate investing. Two and a half years later and with the tremendous efforts of numerous online platforms, online real estate investing is now a reality that is rapidly approaching mainstream status. In this chapter, we will delve into the top ten reasons that we see as to why investors are getting involved.

1 **Online convenience:** The rapid rise of e-commerce shows how people utilize the Internet to buy everything from automobiles to groceries. People like the speed and convenience of being able to access information, compare and contrast choices, form a conclusion and complete a transaction whether they are at home, in an office or poolside at their favorite beach destination. Investors now have that same type of access to institutional-quality commercial real estate offerings literally at their fingertips and in real time.

2 **National Access:** Investors no longer have to focus on real estate deals that they stumble across in their own backyard. In addition, the old school method of real estate investing often relied upon finding out about a potential investment opportunity by word-of-mouth. This method, which is commonly referred to as the "country club model" made access to real estate investments difficult to identify and highly inefficient. Online real estate investing shatters this paradigm by revolutionizing access and delivering transparency to private real estate offerings.

Platforms such as CrowdStreet provide a gateway to access offering information on a wide variety of live deals across the U.S. An investor can access investment opportunities across the country just as easily as in his or her own home city. Investors can now invest in any market of their choice, not just the narrow choice that was previously available to them. At the same time, sponsors can now just as easily accept an investor from across the country as from across town, which has spurred sponsor interest in developing a national, rather than regional, investor base. Access to deals that they, otherwise, would have no knowledge of is a frequent number one reason investors cite as motivation for joining online platforms such as CrowdStreet.

3 **Compare and contrast multiple competing investments:** Now that investors have broad reaching access to private real estate investment opportunities across the country, the next step is to evaluate them. Quality online real estate investing platforms provide comprehensive offering information in an easy to decipher and consistent format. The result is that investors can now quickly compare and contrast competing offerings and filter through them to find a project that fits his or her investment criteria, as well as register to receive notifications when new offerings that match the investor's criteria become available.

"Ready to invest in commercial real estate? Crowdfunding platforms offer a great way to do it."

Ian Formigle

CrowdStreet makes a point to put all of its offering information and documents into the same format. To learn more about how to review an investment offering on the CrowdStreet Marketplace, you can view our video, "How to Review an Investment Offering". Also, keep in mind that in any market, when efficiency, scalability and choice arrives, consumers (or in this case investors) typically win. As the online real estate investing market continues to grow, the quality of investment choices and terms offered to investors will inevitably continue to improve as more investors enter online marketplaces and more sponsors enter and compete to attract them.

4 **Directly invest in commercial real estate:** Online real estate investing allows investors to directly invest in commercial real estate, meaning they are not buying into a publicly traded real estate company that owns dozens of properties, or a mutual fund that includes an assortment of different real estate companies. Rather, direct real estate investment gives investors a stake in one specific property, or a fund with a specific investment focus. Direct investment allows investors to select the specific property type, the location and the operator that best suits their investment strategy and objectives. For more information on this topic, please check out our article, "What are the Differences Between Direct and Indirect (REIT) Real Estate Investments?"

5 **Cash flow:** Most private real estate offerings offer the prospect of sustainable investor cash flow distributions that are targeted to grow over the asset holding period. Often times, these distributions commence at 6% - 9% annualized rates of return, typically paid quarterly, that can hit double digit yields within three years and sometimes even achieve such yields out of the gate. In a yield starved world, investors are increasingly discovering that cash flowing commercial real estate investments provide an attractive option to earn a strong yield as well as equity appreciation upon sale.

6 **Lower minimum investment amounts:** Online real estate investment platforms put direct real estate investment more easily in reach for individual investors. In the past, the ability to invest in a real estate private offering usually came with a minimum investment amount of $100,000 or greater. Now investors can access institutional quality real estate offerings for as little as $10,000.

7 **Diversification:** Modern Portfolio Theory posits that diversification is key to achieving optimal returns, while also providing some protection against exposure to market risks (for more information on this topic, please see our chapter "Invest like Harvard: How to Profit from Direct Real Estate Investing"). The relatively low minimum investment amounts made possible by online real estate investing platforms, allow individual investors, for the first time, to mimic the endowment model of investing and quickly build a diversified real estate investment portfolio. Rather than sinking $100,000 into a single property and waiting for it to reach maturity, investors can now choose to invest $10,000 or $20,000 into five to 10

different deals that vary by geographic regions, sponsors, investment structures, asset classes, risk profiles and holding periods. To learn more about the rapid diversification now available through real estate investing online, please read our chapter," How to Build a Diversified Real Estate Portfolio Using CrowdFunded Real Estate".

8 **Robust reporting platforms:** Online real estate investing platforms offer online dashboards that help investors to manage their investments, regardless of whether it is a single property or a larger portfolio of real estate assets. Investors can use their dashboard for a variety of functions, such as to access quarterly reports, store all investor documents, receive and store K-1s and view distributions. CrowdStreet, for example, is continually adding new tools to our investor dashboard to that, in its next iteration, will now include robust portfolio analytics.

The explosive growth occurring in the real estate crowdfunding industry validates why investors are being increasingly drawn to the space. Title II of the Jumpstart our Business Startups or "JOBS" Act, passed in September of 2013, provided the catalyst for the emergence of online marketplaces dedicated to direct real estate investing. Two and a half years later and with the tremendous efforts of numerous online platforms, online real estate investing is now a reality that is rapidly approaching mainstream status. In this chapter, we will delve into the top ten reasons that we see as to why investors are getting involved.

9 **Dissatisfaction with equity markets:** Another factor that is enticing investors to move into direct real estate investing is a growing dissatisfaction and concern over exposure to equity markets. From domestic markets at all-time highs yet with international distress over uncertainty in China, a political roller coaster and negative interest rates (see our recent article: Negative Interest Rates' Effects on U.S. Real Estate, investors have been exiting the U.S. equity markets and redeploying capital into direct real estate investments. In a climate of heightened uncertainty, a well-leased commercial real estate asset with a durable rent roll increasingly looks like an attractive alternative.

10 **It's the same as it has always been; just better:** Finally, and perhaps most important, is that the advent of online real estate investing is a story of modality and not one of a fundamental change in action or structure. Once investors understand this story, skepticism subsides and the virtues of online investing platforms begin to shine.

For example, a common myth that is debunked as soon as investors better understand online real estate investing, is that it is different or riskier than offline real estate investing. Online real estate investing is syndication. Syndication, in its purest form, is a pooling of individuals to invest jointly into something that no individual could afford to invest in alone.

Syndication has existed offline for centuries if not millennia. As mentioned above, prior to the passage of Title II of the JOBS Act in September of 2013, U.S. security regulations mandated that syndication be conducted privately pursuant to Section 506(b) of Regulation D. Since the passage of Title II, syndication can be conducted publicly pursuant to Section 506(c) of Regulation D. Now that syndication can be conducted publicly it can occur online. Now that it can occur online, it can allow technology companies to emerge (such as CrowdStreet) to make it more efficient, scalable and transparent.

Every investment opportunity applying for inclusion to the CrowdStreet Marketplace is subjected to a rigorous, objective vetting process. Only 2% of all applicants successfully pass this process and appear on CrowdStreet's marketplace. For an in-depth description of the CrowdStreet vetting process please view our CrowdStreet Marketplace Screening Process video.

Putting it all together

Investors who study the space of online real estate investing are beginning to recognize the power it possesses to revolutionize their portfolio strategy. Tapping into the true power of direct real estate investing requires leveraging the tools, resources and efficiencies of the online real estate marketplace. The more investors who enter the marketplace, the better the marketplace becomes.

Commercial real estate investment has historically been limited to deep-pocketed investors, typically those with a minimum $250,000 to invest in each deal. Thanks to the JOBS Act and new software which enables real estate syndications at scale, CrowdStreet is now able to provide access to institutional-quality commercial real estate investment offerings with minimums as low as $10,000.

What is Real Estate Syndication?

Crowdfunding is harnessing the power of technology to modernize the centuries-old practice of real estate syndication and, in the process, is putting institutional quality real estate deals at the fingertips of today's investors. In this chapter we give a brief history of real estate syndication including an in-depth view on its most modern incarnation, real estate crowdfunding. We also give details on how both investors and qualified sponsors can learn more about this technology-enabled future of real estate investing.

Crowdfunding is harnessing the power of technology to modernize the centuries-old practice of real estate syndication and, in the process, is putting institutional quality real estate deals at the fingertips of today's investors.

A real estate syndicate is a group of investors who pool their capital to buy or build property. Combined, individuals and companies have more buying power than what they could manage on their own. Syndicates are commonly structured as special-purpose entities, such as limited

Partnerships ("LPs") or limited liability companies ("LLCs"). Despite the legal form it takes, a special purpose entity is the method by which investors purchase the real estate, such as an apartment complex, office building or even a portfolio or property fund.

"In this section, I define syndication, cover a bit of its history and explain why it is commonly utilized as a means to capitalize real estate private equity offerings."

Ian Formigle

A Brief History of Real Estate Syndication

The practice of teaming up to acquire real estate has a long history that goes back hundreds of years, but for most of the 20th Century it has been relatively clandestine. It used to be that real estate entrepreneurs (now known as "sponsors") could advertise their investment ideas to anyone; the term of art for this practice today is "public solicitation". However, the Securities Act of 1933 required all new securities offerings to be registered with the Securities Exchange Commission ("SEC") so that the federal body could provide oversight and protect investors from fraud. Of course, registering each offering and jumping through the necessary hoops made syndication far less efficient.

Public vs. Private Syndication

Luckily, though, the SEC promulgated "safe harbor" rules that allowed for sponsors to avoid registration under certain conditions. However, the safe harbors did not allow for public solicitation. Therefore, sponsors had two choices: 1.) raise money without public solicitation and avoid registration, or 2.) register the securities with the SEC, wait for approval, and then solicit investments from the public. The prior is almost always more efficient for sponsors, and therefore they almost always choose private syndication.

Although the Securities Act of 1933 effectively stopped public solicitation, private syndication continued. Such deals forced syndicators to gather capital from their own private "black book" of moneyed sources that often included members of the country club set, family trusts and working professionals, among others. Those real estate syndications were put together quietly and relied heavily on personal connections or brokers.

One notable example of the power of syndication dates back to the early 1960s when a group came together to acquire the Empire State Building in New York City. Syndicators reportedly sold about 3,300 ownership shares at $10,000 each to own a piece of the prestigious 102-story building, which at the time was one of the tallest buildings in the world.

Modern Day Syndication: Crowdfunding

These days, crowdfunding firms are writing a new chapter in the evolution of real estate syndications. The Jumpstart Our Business Startups ("JOBS") Act of 2012 directed the SEC to allow public solicitation without registration so long as all purchasers are accredited. Hence, we have Rule 506(c) which does just that. The JOBS Act is widely credited with launching the crowdfunding industry. Effectively, crowdfunding platforms are leveraging online technology to create a new, efficient place for real estate syndication that bridges the gap between syndicators and a much larger pool of investors. Because they can reach a wider audience, sponsors have a tool that enables them to raise capital more quickly and efficiently manage and grow those new relationships. Also, individuals can now easily identify and invest in real estate opportunities anywhere in the country via the online crowdfunding marketplace. Real estate investing via syndications is an established practice with a long track record of delivering results to both sides - syndicators and investors. Crowdfunding firms such as CrowdStreet are simply layering technology on top of that practice to create a new online platform that makes real estate syndication transparent, efficient and scalable for the first time in its history. Online real estate syndication has the potential to launch a new era of real estate investing. That is already evident in a crowdfunding investing platform that has experienced explosive growth in just a few years with even more growth ahead.

CRE Investing Guides

The Definitive Guide to Commercial Real Estate Property Types

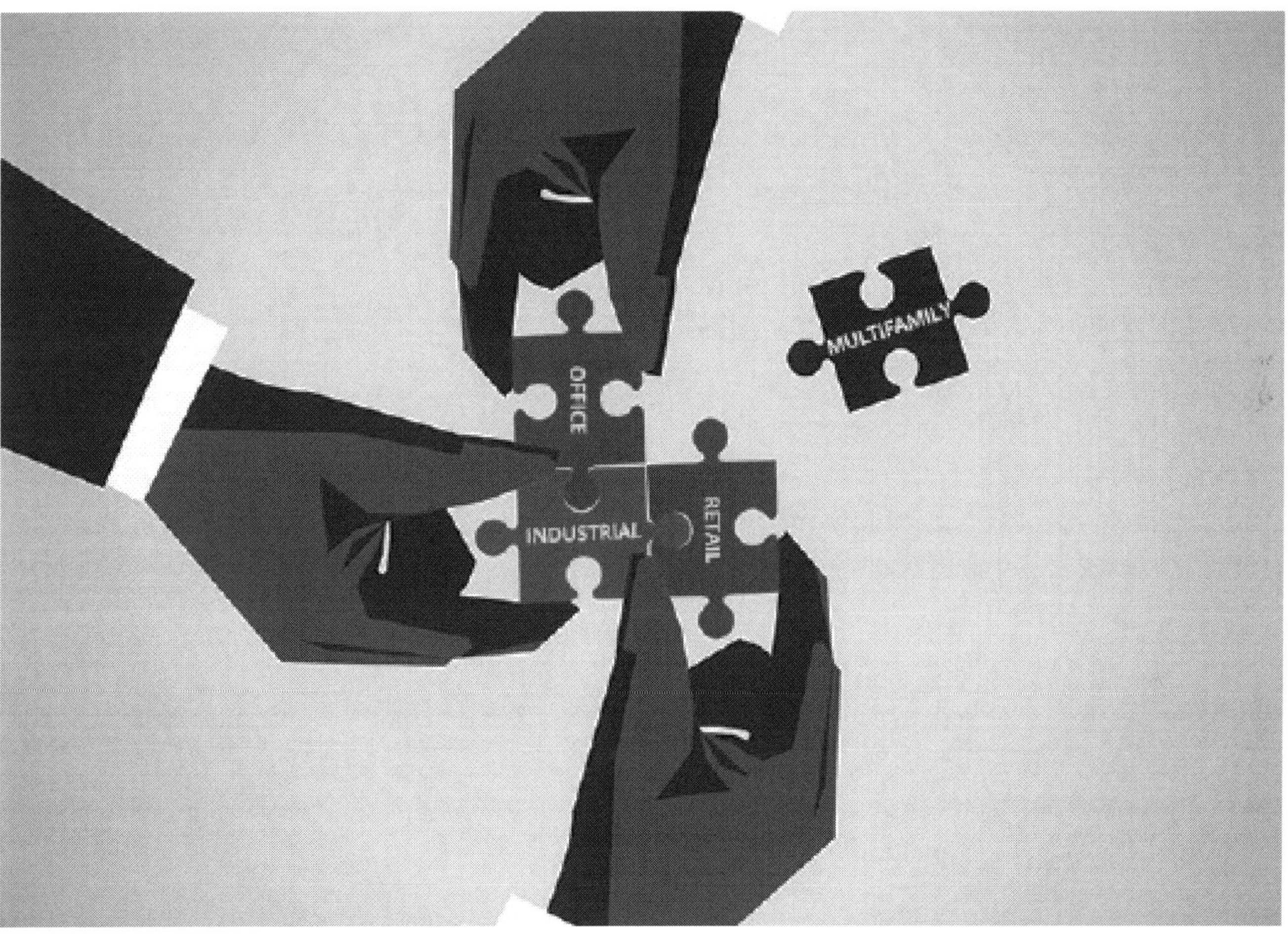

The "four basic food groups" in real estate are generally viewed as office, industrial, retail and multifamily. Each real estate property type (in the industry referred to as 'asset classes') can be further divided into sub-categories. For example, there are more than a half dozen types of retail investment properties. In addition, there are numerous other property types outside of the core four, including hotels, self-storage, medical office, senior housing, student housing and land, among others. Finally, nearly every property type can be divided by quality, labeled as Class A, B, or C. In this chapter we give a detailed overview of the multitude of real estate property types/sub-categories/quality-types as well details on how to apply this information to get started in CRE investing.

Commercial real estate was long considered an "alternative asset" class that floated on the periphery of traditional investments such as stocks, bonds and mutual funds. In recent years, commercial real estate has increasingly migrated into the mainstream as a sought after asset. This migration has been reinforced by the fact that professional investors have used it heavily in portfolio allocations for decades and that commercial real estate often outperforms all other asset classes (see "Invest Like Harvard: The Advantages of Direct Real Estate Investing"). Add to this level of performance the additional fact that commercial real estate is the third largest asset class (after stocks and bonds) and now a compelling case emerges for inclusion of direct real estate investments into any portfolio. As investors are now discovering and embracing direct real estate investments as an enviable part of an investment portfolio, it raises a series of questions on defining subsets within the greater asset class.

> "Understanding the different types of commercial real estate is the starting point for understanding how to successfully invest in it. In this section, I walk you through the different asset class or "food groups" of commercial real estate."
>
> Ian Formigle

Commercial real estate is vast in almost every sense. That is actually good for investors as it provides numerous different entry points into investments, and it enables investors to easily diversify growing real estate portfolios. The "four basic food groups" in real estate are generally viewed as office, industrial, retail and multifamily. Each real estate property type (in the industry referred to as 'asset classes') can be further divided into sub-categories. For example, there are more than a half dozen types of retail investment properties. In addition, there are numerous other property types outside of the core four, including hotels, self-storage, medical office, senior housing, student housing and land, among others. Finally, nearly every property type can be divided by quality, labeled as Class A, B, or C. Some of the main real estate property types are described below.

Office

Office buildings come in all shapes and sizes from 100-story glass and steel towers in Manhattan to a one-story bricker in Des Moines. Office properties are generally distinguished by height, location, and use.

The height classes that have been adopted by Colliers and NAIOP, one of the largest commercial real estate industry organizations in the country, are as follows:

Low-rise: <7 stories

Mid-rise: 7-25 stories

High-rise: 25+ stories

The tenants that office buildings attract may, in some cases, depend upon the height. Consider that certain office users, such as law firms, like office space with views that can impress clients and attract top talent. Conversely, creative tech users often prefer immediate access to their office space to park a bike or bring a dog and therefore don't generally like to be in an office tower that probably shares space with "old economy" tenants, such as that law firm, especially if the creative user feels the vibe of the building is stiff. While office space is evolving, it's still a challenge to have people in suits, bikes and dogs share the same elevators. Furthermore, these structures will vary in materials, cost to construct, and maintenance issues.

The next office classification, location, consists of two types: Central Business District ("CBD") and suburban. While you might find the full spectrum of heights in the CBD, lower rents in the suburbs generally do not support the most costly construction techniques that high-rise and even most low-rise buildings require. Tenants attracted to CBD offices tend to be more established professional service or tech firms, while smaller or more emerging groups will be attracted to the relatively low rents found in the suburbs.

Finally, office buildings vary by use. The most common is general office use, with primarily tech and professional services tenants. General office buildings will have few specialized tenant improvements. Medical office, another office subtype, will attract primarily medical tenants, such as doctors' offices and hospitals. These properties might have significant tenant improvements to accommodate specialized equipment, hazards, and privacy; therefore, they may be harder to convert to general office in the event that a major tenant moves out. Finally, some space in an office building may be used for heavier, more industrial or technological uses. This is known as flex space. Overall, at least 75% of a building's interior space needs to be designed and finished as office space in order to qualify as an office property type according to NAIOP. This distinction becomes important when reading about market trends. Office categories are
defined in more detail by the Building Owners and Managers Association International (BOMA) and NAIOP

For more detailed information on office please see our chapter "Investing in Office Real Estate."

Industrial

Industrial buildings are used for functions such as manufacturing, R&D and the storage and distribution of goods. The three main categories are manufacturing, warehouse and Flex/R&D, which are defined as follows by the National Association of Industrial & Office Parks (NAIOP):

Manufacturing: A facility used for the conversion, fabrication and/or assembly of raw or partly wrought materials into products/goods. These properties tend to have less than 20% office space and can be further classified for a heavy or light industrial use.

Warehouse: A facility primarily used for the storage and/or distribution of materials, goods and merchandise. These buildings tend to have less than 15% office space, and modern facilities have high clear ceiling heights that allow for more cubic storage space. This category also may include specialty facilities, such as cold or freezer storage for food.

Flex/R&D: These industrial buildings are designed to give its occupants flexibility in use of the space. Sometimes referred to as flex/tech space, these buildings are an office-industrial hybrid that can have 30% to even 100% office finish.

Because they require a lot of acreage for wide building footprints, low-density parking, and truck turning, industrial buildings are almost never found in the CBD. Therefore, it is rare to hear them distinguished according to anything other than use.

For more detailed information on industrial please see our chapter: "Investing in Industrial Real Estate."

Retail

Retail property types range from single-tenant buildings, such as a Walgreens, to large megamalls. High-rise buildings are almost never used solely for retail; instead, only a portion of a high-rise building, typically at ground level, will be used as a retail component. Retail centers that have more than a single tenant are grouped by size and tenant type. The International Council of Shopping Centers (ICSC), the largest retail industry organization in the world, defines different types of shopping centers as follows:

Malls: Regional malls range in size from about 400,000 to 800,000 square feet and include inline retail, service and restaurant tenants, as well as major department store anchors, such as Macy's and Nordstrom. Super regional malls are upwards of 800,000 square feet.

Community & Neighborhood Centers: These centers include a mix of general merchandise or convenience-oriented tenants. Oftentimes, these centers are "anchored" by a big box retailer such as Target, Walmart or a grocery store. These centers might range in size from 30,000 to 400,000 square feet.

Strip centers: Named for their straight configuration, these centers generally focus on convenience tenants such as dry cleaners, nail salons and sandwich shops. Strip centers are smaller than 30,000 square feet.

Power centers: These centers are dominated by "big box" retailers such as Best Buy, Dick's Sporting Goods and Bed Bath & Beyond with only a few small tenants.

Lifestyle Centers: As enclosed malls became too expensive to build, it created a new generation of open-air lifestyle centers that feature upscale apparel and other retailers, along with dining and entertainment.

One of the most important aspects of the retail subtype is its dependency upon traffic and parking. Urban retail spaces, which usually are a portion of a mixed-use building rather than a single-use building, rely heavily upon foot traffic, while strip centers rely heavily upon vehicle traffic. Lifestyle centers, on the other hand, will create their own traffic because the anchor tenants are usually "destination tenants," such as movie theaters and restaurants. Except for the most densely urban locations, almost all retail tenants require certain minimum parking to square footage ratios in order to lease space.

Another important feature of retail properties is tenant mix. While multifamily and office tenants generally do not care who their neighbors are as long as they are quiet, retail tenants thrive off certain neighbors and refuse to be located near others, usually competitors. For example, you may commonly find a Jo-Ann Fabrics located in the same shopping center as a Big Lots or a Dollar Tree. This strategy is referred to as adjacencies. Having an appropriate tenant mix is something of an art in the retail industry.

For more detailed information on retail please see our chapter: "Investing in Retail Real Estate."

Multifamily

Apartment properties also come in all shapes and sizes, ranging from dense, high-rise, urban apartment buildings to sprawling, resort-style complexes in the suburbs complete with swimming pools, fitness centers and outdoor patios.

In terms of size, multifamily buildings are often classified as follows:

Low Rise or Garden Style: 2-4 stories high

Mid Rise: 5-9 stories

High Rise: 10 stories or higher

In previous years, multifamily properties were regarded less as commercial real estate assets and more closely associated with other residential assets such as single family homes. However, in recent years as the US has increasingly urbanized and multifamily properties have become more institutional in nature with costly design and vast amenities and now increasingly owned by some of the nation's largest institutional investors, multifamily is now firmly cemented as one of the four primary commercial real estate asset classes (the other primary three being office, industrial and retail).

For more detailed information on multifamily please see our chapter: "Investing in Multifamily Real Estate."

Hotels

Hotels are defined primarily by the services and amenities that they offer. Another key distinction in this category is the "flag" or operating brand that includes the likes of Holiday Inn, Hilton and Marriott among others. The three main types of hotels include:

Full-Service: These hotels are loaded with guest services and amenities, such as on-site restaurants, banquet and meeting rooms, concierge service, spas and retail shops. Some examples include the Hyatt, Ritz-Carlton, St. Regis and Westin. For full service hotels, the overall success of the hotel is highly sensitive to the quality of its onsite amenities, particularly the food and beverage services.

Limited-Service: These properties are a step down in terms of service and amenities, often including meeting rooms, a fitness center and a swimming pool. As a result, the operations of this class of hotel are more predictable in comparison to full-service hotels. Some examples include Fairfield Inn, Hampton Inn and Holiday Inn Express.

Budget: These "no frills" hotels may offer one or two guest services or amenities, but they tend to focus on providing the basic necessities for a very low rate. Examples include EconoLodge, Super 8 and Starwood's Aloft.

For more information on hospitality please see our chapter: "Investing in Hotel Real Estate."

Senior Housing

The aging baby boomer population is attracting more investment capital into this sector in terms of acquisitions, development and property renovations. The National Investment Center for the Seniors Housing & Care Industry (NIC) is an industry association that offers a variety of research and resources for investors, owners and operators. The different categories of seniors housing facilities include:

Independent Living: Designed for seniors who require little or no assistance. These properties often cater to residents who are 55+ with a variety of on-site amenities and social programming for active seniors.

Assisted Living: These licensed facilities combine housing with a variety of personal support services, such as transportation, meals, laundry and health-care assistance.

Nursing Homes: Properties are generally licensed and provide 24-hour skilled care for chronic and short-term conditions that require medical and nursing care.

Memory care: The long-term care facilities are designed for people with a level of impairment, such as dementia, that makes it unsafe for them to continue to stay at home, but who do not require the intensive care of a skilled nursing facility.

For more information on senior housing please see our chapter: "Investing in Senior Housing Real Estate."

Self-Storage

Self-storage is a segment of the real estate market that has continued to evolve in the past decade. The traditional rural and suburban properties with gravel driveways and roll-up metal doors are being replaced with modern facilities and sophisticated operators.

Developers have been busy building and converting urban, multi-story properties that feature climate and humidity-controlled space and high-tech security systems. In addition to providing storage to individual and business customers, some facilities also offer specialty storage for boats, classic cars, wine and documents.

For more information on self-storage please see our chapter: "Investing in Self Storage Real Estate."

Single-family Residential (in bulk)

The housing market crash helped to bring a wave of opportunistic investors into the single family rental market. Investors bought homes at a discount and converted them to rental properties to serve a growing population of renters. This niche market now includes institutional investors and REITs, as well as professional property managers that oversee the rentals and day-to-day operations of these properties.

Making the Grade in Real Estate: Understanding Class A B and C

Commercial real estate applies a simple grading system to assets to rate overall quality and key characteristics. Buildings are classified as A, B or C, and that ranking is an important indicator to gauge a property's competitive position in a marketplace and where it fits in relation to market value and rents. In this chapter we walk you through the different property classes and highlight the investment opportunities specific to each.

Commercial real estate applies a simple grading system to assets to rate overall quality and key characteristics. Buildings are classified as A, B or C, and that ranking is an important indicator to gauge a property's competitive position in a marketplace and where it fits in relation to market value and rents.

Building class applies to all property types – industrial, retail, apartments and hotels among others. Although by no means definitive, some of the accepted descriptions for the three different classes are as follows:

Class A Properties

This is the top tier in a particular market. Some of the key attributes of Class A properties include high-end construction and interior finishes, modern architectural design, state-of-the-art mechanical systems and technology and a variety of property amenities. For example, Class A office amenities might include valet parking, bike storage and locker room facilities, an on-site restaurant or coffee bar and the latest in sustainable design. Class A multifamily properties in suburban locations, will almost always offer near resort-like settings complete with fountains, lavish pools, barbeque areas and fitness centers. Class A properties are best-in-class assets that usually command the highest possible rents in their respective submarkets.

Class B Properties

Class B properties are a step down from Class A in terms of building quality, location and amenities. While it is possible to have a brand new Class B asset, it is far more common that an asset becomes Class B due to age. Class B buildings are typically at least in good, if not great, condition and may achieve above average rents, but rents and property values are lower in comparison to their Class A competitors. Also of note, historic assets (even if well maintained) are often rated Class B due to physical aspects that, while charming, are technically outmoded (e.g. single pane windows, small elevator cabs and lower ceiling heights). More specific to retail shopping centers, the quality of the tenant mix also can influence the class status for the entire property.

> "Once you understand the different types of real estate, you are ready to move on to learning how it is classified (graded). In this section, I walk you through explanations of the three primary classifications that are applied to all types of commercial real estate."

Ian Formigle

Class C Properties

This is the lowest rated tier and least desirable of buildings. Spaces within Class C assets are barely functional and are cheap to rent. Oftentimes, these are older assets that have outdated building systems, design or finishes, or they may be in desperate need of maintenance and renovations. Many Class C properties are in the waning days of their useful life and may be rapidly approaching functional obsolescence. For example, modern warehouse facilities are built with clear ceiling heights of 34 to 36 feet – about twice as high as was the norm back in the 1960s and 1970s. Companies such as Amazon want the biggest, tallest box to accommodate more efficient storage of goods. Some of the older warehouse facilities are simply not adequate for many of today's tenants. Due to these types of constraints, Class C operators are often relegated to minimizing operating costs as a primary strategy since their revenue upside is limited. While a stock of real estate exists below Class C, it is generally not of investable quality and, therefore, does not require classification.

Classifications are Subject to Change

Another important factor to note is that buildings can move down or up in classification. As mentioned above, a new building with state of the art amenities may easily start out as a Class A property but it may slip to Class B over time as the building ages, tenant preferences change or trade areas within a submarket shift. Conversely, it is possible to move a property up in class (e.g. from Class C to Class B or from Class B to Class A) through renovation and tenant repositioning. This is precisely the scenario that value-added investors seek where they can acquire a Class B or Class C property, make the necessary improvements or renovations and elevate its status. By doing so, owners boost cash flows, rents, tenant quality and, as a result, overall property values. Finally, retail centers, in particular, are highly location sensitive. A change in infrastructure or access can shift traffic patterns that create new "A" destinations, or even turn a previous premier location into a less desirable "C" location.

Cyclical Factors

Once you understand the definition of asset classifications, it is important to contemplate how demand for each class of an asset type changes depending upon cyclical factors. Take, for example, the multifamily asset class. Class A properties can face two states of flux depending upon market and economic conditions. During periods of strong economic growth, Class A owners may find their turnover rates to be higher than normal as their best tenants vacate to buy homes, which are absorbed by former Class B tenants that are ready to step up to Class A living. During recessionary periods, Class A owners often increase concessions and even lower rents to retain tenants who, otherwise, may look to move down to a Class B property to save money. It is due to these types of cyclical effects that Class B multifamily properties are often viewed as desirable investments because, regardless of the economic cycle, Class B assets benefit from their middle market position, meaning that there is usually an even balance of tenants entering and exiting the asset class.

Asset Class and Returns are not Correlated

In most cases, asset class and returns are not correlated. However, to the extent that loose correlation may exist, it's usually inverse. As one of my former colleagues would humorously (but accurately) point out when evaluating a potential Class C acquisition, "we've made more money over the years owning junkyards than museums". More important is knowing where a property fits within the asset class ranking system and where it is headed given a particular business plan. This helps to put investment opportunities into context in relation to potential risks and returns. In most commercial real estate markets, demand exists for all three classes of assets - the key is validating that a targeted property acquisition is competitive within its asset class and will remain so over the course of the holding period.

At a glance, the asset class system seems artless. Yet those categories can be subjective and also can vary widely depending on the individual market or region. For example, a Class A office building in a tertiary market may be viewed as a Class B building in a primary market such as New York City or Los Angeles. In addition, once assets reach the edge of a classification tier, they lose consensus when it comes to ranking them. Some might consider an asset as Class A- while others might view it as Class B+. The more an investor compares and contrasts competing assets, the better he or she becomes at calling the bluff of an overrated fringe asset or having confidence that a property is easily bumped to the next classification tier with the right amount of refurbishment.

How to Invest in Class A and Class B Real Estate with $10,000

Investors will typically find offerings of Class A and Class B properties on the CrowdStreet Marketplace. While CrowdStreet may accept Class C properties, it will typically only do so if the business plan includes a robust asset improvement component that will reposition the property to Class B status.

The Four Phases of the Real Estate Cycle

Similar to the broader economy, commercial real estate is a cyclical market. There are four phases to the real estate cycle: Recovery, Expansion, Hypersupply and Recession. One of the unique aspects of real estate is that people can invest successfully across all four phases of the cycle. However, understanding whether a cycle is climbing closer to a market peak, or starting down the slippery slope towards a market low can often mean the difference between a successful investment and a significant loss. In this chapter we outline the four phases of the real estate market and provide strategies for successful investments at each stage.

Similar to the broader economy, commercial real estate is a cyclical market. There are four phases to the real estate cycle:

Recovery

Expansion

Hyper Supply

Recession

The four phases move in a continuous wave pattern that looks like this:

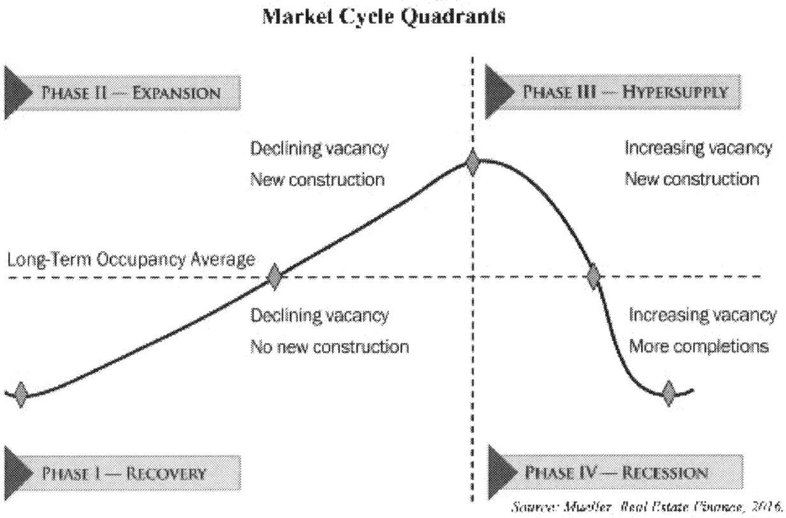

Source: Mueller, Real Estate Finance, 2016.

Depicted above is a single cycle. The end of the recession phase connects to the beginning of the recovery phase to form the continuous wave pattern.

As we begin, I want to give special thanks to our friend Dr. Glenn Mueller of the University of Denver for his thought leadership in this space. Any investor who wishes to do a deeper dive on real estate cycles is advised to check out Dr. Mueller's outstanding work.

Understanding the progression of each phase within the cycle is critical in being able to identify investment opportunities, as well as risks that can arise, with heightened sensitivity when phases are on the verge of transitioning.

One of the unique aspects of commercial real estate is that investors can invest successfully across all four phases of the cycle. However, understanding whether a cycle is climbing closer to a market peak, or starting down the slippery slope towards a market low can affect a variety of factors, such as:

- **Pairing investment strategy to phase**
- **Holding periods and exit strategies**
- **Return expectations**
- **Performance as it relates to income and appreciation**
- **Timing of capital improvements**

In this chapter, we describe each of the four phases and highlight certain appropriate investing strategies for each phase.

Phase 1: Recovery

The recovery phase is the bottom of the trough. Occupancies are likely at or near their low point with tepid demand for space and minimal leasing velocity. There is usually no new construction underway and rental rate growth is either still negative to flat or, later in the phase, possibly occurring, but at levels that are below the rate of inflation. Identifying the beginning of the recovery phase is difficult as the market still feels like it is in recession.

Strategies:

Opportunistic: Provided you move early in the phase, there are still opportunities to buy bargain-priced properties in varying states of distress and begin to reposition those assets as the recovery phase takes hold. Holding periods are often targeted at two to four years with a business plan that contemplates transitioning the subject acquisition out of its current state of distress and liquidating during the expansion phase once the property achieves a core-plus to value-add profile.

Value-add: Value-add strategies during a recovery phase require careful thought and patience. For example, while pricing may provide for a great basis in a value-add asset during the early to mid portion of a recovery phase, the business plan should include contingencies for execution since strong lease up may not occur until the early part of the expansion phase.

Core: Investing in core properties during the recovery phase can be a highly profitable strategy, particularly if the targeted asset has a significant amount of lease roll over the ensuing two to four years. A typical strategy for a core asset in a recovery phase will be to acquire a trophy asset in a "main and main" location and then capitalize on the strong rental growth of the next cycle through a combination of lease renewals and lease up of any residual vacancy from the previous recession phase. The asset is then primely positioned to be refinanced or sold during the expansion phase.

Phase 2: Expansion

During the expansion phase, the market is on the upswing in terms of growing demand for space. From a macroeconomic perspective, GDP growth is back to normal levels and quarterly job growth is strong. Occupancy rates are improving and rents are on the rise. Rents now approach levels that can justify new construction, and in certain very tight markets, surge ahead at break-neck speeds. Development activity begins to return during the expansion phase. There also is a high point during the expansion phase – the crest of the wave – where supply and demand is in equilibrium.

Strategies:

Development: This is the ideal time to develop or redevelop properties, because the current demand for space and leasing momentum helps properties stabilize more quickly upon delivery at rental rates that may set new market highs.

Core-Plus: Investors who seek lower levels of risk can acquire Core-Plus properties knowing they will enjoy high rates of tenant retention with continued rent growth.

Value-add: The expansion phase is prime time for value-add investing. Sophisticated investors can acquire properties with current deficiencies at substantial discounts to stabilized value, invest into capital expenditures and reposition assets rapidly aided by the strong absorption that is inherent to expansion phases of the cycle. Once repositioned, the asset can now command full stabilized value, which may translate into a refinance or sale.

Opportunistic: While most opportunistic opportunities have disappeared by the expansion phase, it may still be possible to find the exception case where a capital starved asset remains in a state of distress. In that event, an opportunistic strategy during an expansion phase can be highly profitable but should accompany a short holding period unless the business plan is to refinance and hold post stabilization.

Phase 3: Hypersupply

The equilibrium between supply and demand in the expansion wave often tips over into excess. Oversupply of space can be caused by overbuilding, or a pullback in demand caused by a shift in the economy. Hypersupply is marked by rising vacancies. Rent growth may remain positive, but at declining levels.

Strategies:

Core: Some investors may decide to sell assets ahead of what they perceive as a coming decline in property values and more challenging leasing market. At the same time, other investors may concur on the macro perspective but instead of liquidity seek opportunities to take shelter from the coming storm. A core property with high occupancy and a rent roll chock full of credit tenants with average remaining lease terms in excess of five years is a prime example of a core property that will perform well through the downturn with lease roll that is optimally timed to occur during the next expansion phase.

Opportunistic: At this phase in cycle, an opportunistic strategy may be more of a pricing strategy that can apply to any asset class rather than a typical distressed asset scenario. For example, once the hypersupply phase has set in, owners who are ill-equipped to operate through the impending recession, may hit the panic button and liquidate assets at prices that end up approaching recession price levels. In this scenario, the buyer leverages its capital superiority position to acquire a solid asset that he/she is confident will ultimately perform well in the next cycle with a recession phase already priced into the deal.

Phase 4: Recession

Supply outweighs demand, which produces higher vacancies. Rent growth during recession is either negative or at levels that are below the rate of inflation. In addition, operators often resort to offering more concessions and rent reductions to entice and retain tenants.

Strategies:

Opportunistic: This is an ideal time buy distressed assets at steep discounts to replacement cost. It is during the recession phase that buyers will also have the highest probability of acquiring assets in distressed scenarios such as special servicers and lender foreclosures, which are commonly referred to as real estate owned or "REOs". This strategy focuses on absolute basis with a patient and well-capitalized business plan that, when the recovery phase emerges and the sun begins to shine again, the acquirer will then commence repositioning the asset with hopes of disposing of it during the end of the recovery phase or early expansion phase.

Once you understand the four phases of the cycle it then becomes important to begin grasping variances of the four phases.

"Commercial real estate markets are cyclical. In this section, I describe the four phases of commercial real estate cycles and provide insights on optimal strategies for investing at each phase."

Ian Formigle

First, phases do not necessarily occur in equal periods. The recovery phase may be brief and quickly transition to the expansion phase, or it may drag on for years. It's also difficult to project the duration of expansion phases. In addition, cycles can have different total duration. Just because there was general consensus that a previous cycle was nine years doesn't mean that the next cycle will approximate the same total duration.

Second, cycles vary depending on geography and asset class. Certain markets, such as gateway markets, may lead the transition from recession to recovery phases of the next cycle with secondary and tertiary markets to follow suit. Also, different asset classes recover, expand, oversupply and decline at different rates with some of the rate variance attributable to the asset class itself and some of the variance attributable to location both at the metro level and within metros. For example, while overall, the office asset class may be in an expansion phase in a given market, suburban office assets may still be in recovery while urban office may be nearing hypersupply. Therefore, when applying the concept of the four phases of the real estate cycle to a specific asset you must also overlay geographic location and asset class to truly gain a sense of where that asset plots along the cycle wave.

The differences that exist between market timing and performance at different stages of the real estate cycle speak to the importance of creating a diverse real estate investment portfolio to balance out the highs and lows in performance. To that point, CrowdStreet aims to provide a wide variety of real estate investment opportunities across property types and geographic markets.

Investing in Multifamily Real Estate

Multifamily real estate is a widely held and strategic commercial real estate asset class. At roughly 25% of the U.S commercial real estate stock, the multifamily sector now accounts for the second-largest share of institutional investors' real estate holdings, lagging only the office sector. While previously considered a residential asset, multifamily is now firmly cemented as one of the four primary commercial real estate asset classes (the other primary three being office, industrial and retail). In this chapter, we provide an overview of the multifamily asset class, discuss demand drivers, highlight changes in use and conclude with a synthesis of these factors to better equip investors with the knowledge to make informed investment decisions.

Multifamily real estate is a widely held and strategic commercial real estate asset class. At roughly 25% of the U.S commercial real estate stock, the multifamily sector now accounts for the second-largest share of institutional investors' real estate holdings, lagging only the office sector. While previously considered a residential asset, multifamily is now firmly cemented as one of the four primary commercial real estate asset classes (the other primary three being office, industrial and retail).

In this chapter, we provide an overview of the multifamily asset class, discuss demand drivers, highlight changes in use and conclude with a synthesis of these factors to better equip investors with the knowledge to make informed investment decisions.

Asset Class Overview

As an asset class, multifamily spans a wide spectrum of residential properties that technically includes all buildings containing at least two housing units, which are adjacent vertically or horizontally. Multifamily is also characterized by shared physical systems whether it be walls, roofs, heating and cooling, utilities or amenities. While multifamily can include townhouse, condominium and apartment projects, for the purposes of this chapter, we will focus on apartments since they are most commonly acquired as an investment.

Classification: The industry "grades" multifamily properties as Class A, B or C based on criteria such as age, quality, amenities, rent and location among other factors.

Class A multifamily properties, particularly in suburban locations, will almost always offer near resort-like settings complete with fountains, lavish pools, barbeque areas and fitness centers. In general, Class A multifamily properties are best-in-class assets that usually command the highest possible rents in their respective submarkets.

Class B multifamily properties are a step down from Class A in terms of building quality, location and amenities. This property class will often have the term "workforce housing" associated with it as it is often intended to offer a viable housing solution to median wage earners.

Class C multifamily properties are the lowest rated tier of buildings. Spaces within Class C assets are barely functional and are cheap to rent. Often times, these are older assets that have outdated building systems, design or finishes, or they may be in desperate need of maintenance and renovations.

Property Types: Apartment properties also come in all shapes and sizes, ranging from dense, high-rise, urban apartment buildings to sprawling, resort-style complexes in the suburbs complete with swimming pools, fitness centers and outdoor patios. In terms of size and type, multifamily buildings are often classified as follows:

Low Rise or Garden Style: 2-4 stories high and most typically found in suburban locations

Mid Rise: 5-9 stories

High Rise: 10 stories or higher

Demand Drivers

A good way to begin analyzing U.S. multifamily demand drivers is to consider that households are comprised of either owners or renters. According to the U.S. Census Bureau, homeownership, as of March 2016, currently stands at 62.9% (with renters at 37.1%), which is its lowest level in more than 25 years. There are roughly 117.4 million total households:

43.6 Million Renters (37.1%)
73.8 Million Owners (62.9%)
117.4 Million U.S. Households

Demand drivers, for the most part, will 1) increase or decrease the total number of the U.S. households 2) change the percentage breakout of renters vs. owners or 3) both. While there are myriad factors that contribute to multifamily demand, the following comprise the key drivers:

Population Growth: As the population grows, so too will total households albeit at a lower rate. For example, if the U.S. population grew by 5%, which in turn, grew total households by 2.5%, from the 117.4 million noted above, we would now have 120.3 million households. Holding the 62.9% / 37.1% distribution constant would result in an increase in renter households of about 1 million:

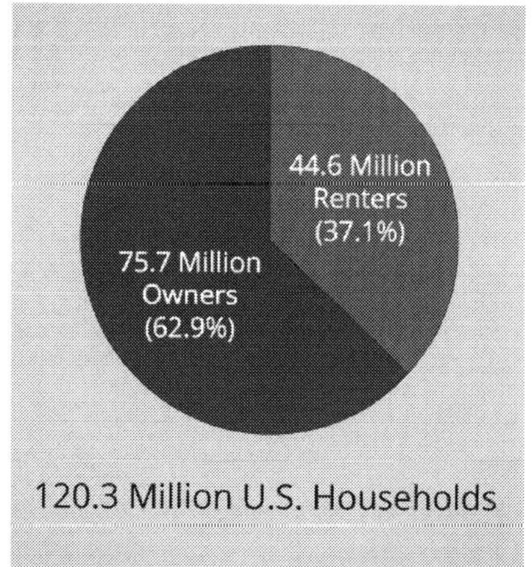

120.3 Million U.S. Households

Rental Household Growth: Following the great recession, we saw homeownership decline from its 2004 peak of 69% to its current level of 62.9%. In this kind of shift, if we hold total households constant, we have more renter households at the expense of fewer owner households. If we use our current U.S. household total of 117.4 million, an owner to renter shift of that magnitude would result in a loss of 7.2 million owner households and an equal gain of 7.2 million renter households. While we know that total households actually changed over this period, this example is designed to illustrate how swings in renters vs. owners affect demand holding total households constant:

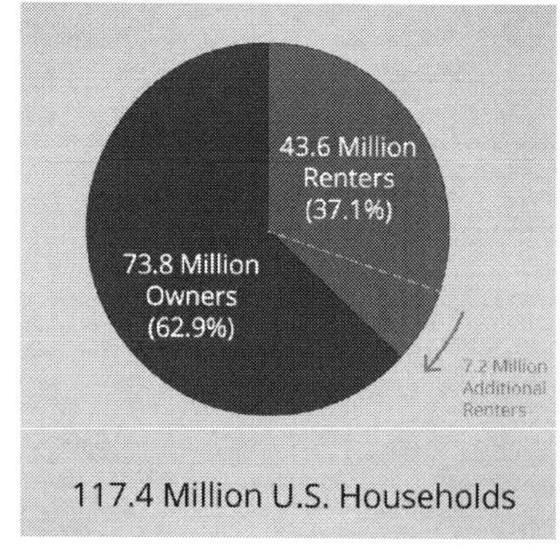

117.4 Million U.S. Households

Job Growth: Job growth correlates to household growth, as people can now afford their own residences (e.g. Millenials that moved out of their parents' homes once they got jobs during the recovery). While job growth grows total U.S. households, it predominantly grows it via renters, since the people who primarily benefit from job growth are generally renters and not owners. Let's consider the following exercise. According to the Bureau of Labor Statistics, the U.S. created 2.7 million jobs in 2015. Let's assume that for every four jobs created one household was formed holding population constant. This assumption would yield 675,000 new households. Let's further assume that 80% of these new households were renters not owners. That would yield 540,000 new renter households and 135,000 new owner households. As a result, 2.7 million new jobs would both grow total households as well as slightly increase the percentage of renters in comparison to owners. If we started with our current 117.4 million U.S. households, it would look like this:

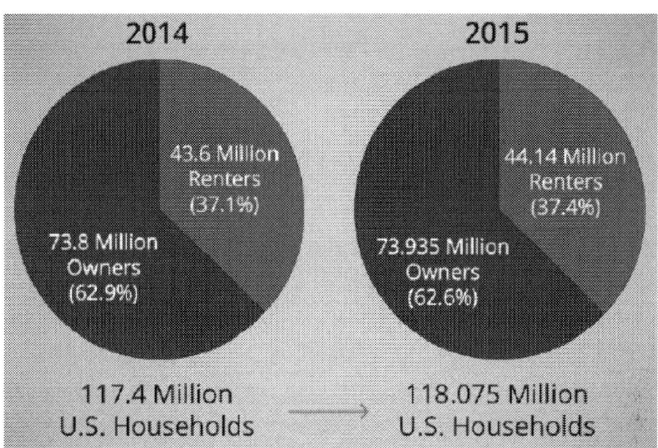

Cost of Ownership: Cost of ownership can be analyzed in two primary ways. First, high real estate prices serve as as a deterrent to ownership since it makes purchasing a residence difficult to afford. As a result, you will see higher percentages of renters in any market where housing stock is expensive. In fact, while the U.S. owner to renter ratio is 62.9% / 37.1% at the national level, it is nearly the inverse in metros such as New York, San Francisco and Los Angeles. When the comparative cost of renting vs. owning changes, it induces demand for the option that just became a bit cheaper. For example, when we see rapid spikes in real estate values, particularly ones that dramatically outpace wage growth, we can expect to see the renter percentage in that location increase and the ownership percentage decrease. Such a change doesn't grow the household number but, rather swings the percentage breakout:

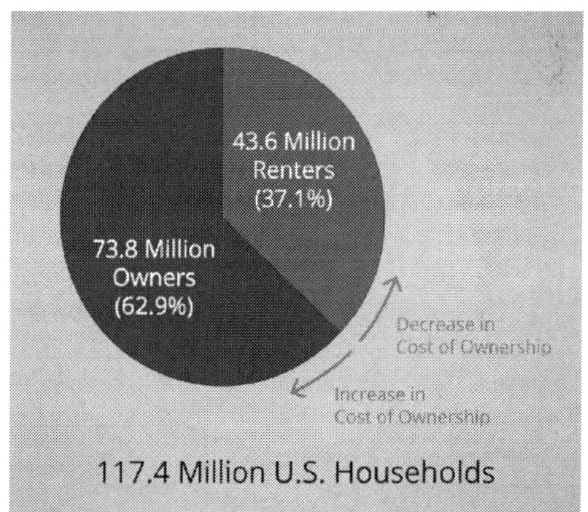

Demographics

Demographic trends have made their own contribution to the growing popularity of renting. The behavior and choices of different demographics has direct effects on the multifamily trends, and now more than ever. According to a study published by the Joint Center for Housing Studies of Harvard University, the increase of 9 million renter households the U.S. has experienced since 2005 is the largest increase in any 10 year period on record.

The aging of the millennial generation (born 1985–2004) is one key demographic trend that has lifted the number of adults in their 20s, the stage of life when renting is most common. Millennials, as a demographic, are delaying marriage, children and moving to the suburbs to buy a home until later in life. This effect has expanded the year-over-year renter pool nationwide. Millennials also are carrying a higher load of student debt in comparison to previous decades, which makes it more challenging to finance a first-time home purchase.

Millenials are not the only demographic making choices in favor of multifamily. Empty nesters are downsizing and opting for low-maintenance rental townhomes and apartments. In addition, both Millenials and empty nesters have been drawn to the urban renaissance movement that is seeing people move back to city centers to live, work and play. This movement is creating more demand for apartment and condo rentals in and around busy downtown and central business districts.

In combination, these trends have boosted the numbers of renters in all age, income, and household categories. Millennials have pushed up the number of renters under age 30 by nearly 1 million over the past decade, while members of generation X (born 1965–1984) added 3 million to the ranks of renters in their 30s and 40s, even though the population in this age range declined. The largest increase, however, was a 4.3 million jump in the number of renters in their 50s and 60s. This growth reflects the aging of baby-boomer renters (born 1946–1964) as well as declines in homeownership rates among this generation. While households in their 20s make up the single largest share, households aged 40 and over now account for a majority of all renters.

Changes in Multifamily Use

Many of the demographic trends, as mentioned above, have led to a number of shifts in multi-family use as the next generation of multifamily developments aims to provide a modern living experience. The following are highlights of the factors changing where apartments are located and what they look like:

Walkable / Bikeable locations: In conjunction with the urban renaissance, renters now desire their apartment to be located in close proximity to neighborhood grocery stores, cafes, pubs and restaurants. In decades past, it was more common to see a multifamily property tucked away in a secure and private setting but that trend has given way to the walkable, bikeable property.

Transit-oriented developments: As commuting via public transportation has become increasingly popular amongst the renter sect, we are seeing more apartment buildings pop up along transit lines. Transit-oriented properties command higher rents and can expect to maintain higher occupancies all things being equal amongst its competitive set.

Modern amenities: With properties that are increasingly walkable and bikeable, renters now desire a host of modern amenities. According to a 2015 nationwide survey conducted by the NMHC, the following are highlights of what renters desired most:

- Bicycle parking
- Rooftop lounges
- Fast internet connections
- Sound proof walls
- In-unit washing machines and dryers
- Balconies

While not top ten in polling, the following are additional modern amenities that renters also seek out:

- Dog washing stations
- Bicycle mechanic stations
- Interior storage units adjacent to dwelling units
- Package lockers

As many new buildings contain most or even all of these types of amenities, the modern apartment building can almost feel like a hotel in the level of service and breadth of amenities offered. It's a far cry from the standard walk up apartment building of the past.

New Development vs. Existing Product

Due to recent changes in use, the amount of new apartment construction nationwide and the current disparity between the cost to build vs. the cost to acquire, many investors are seeking out opportunities to invest in multifamily development rather than multifamily acquisitions. Some of the key points to consider when weighing development vs. acquisition investment opportunities include:

Development risk premium: Investors should be compensated for taking on greater risk associated with development. One rule of thumb is to receive a cap rate premium of 150 basis points or greater on development over acquiring an existing property in order to make it worthwhile for taking on the extra risk (e.g. a brand new property that would currently trade a 4.5% cap rate at stabilization is developed to a 6% or greater operating cap rate at stabilization on cost). As that spread narrows or increases, it creates less or greater incentive to invest in development.

> "Multifamily has been the darling asset class of the current real estate cycle. In this section, I provide an overview of the asset class, discuss demand drivers, highlight recent changes in use and point out the differences in strategy when investing in new construction vs. existing assets."
>
> 
> Ian Formigle

Construction type: Multifamily development can take many forms with varying levels of cost. Construction type and finish levels are the key determinants of price per square foot building costs, which in turn influences the rents a property needs to achieve to hit its target returns. That list ranging from low to high building cost includes:

Stick built: The least expensive building style uses primarily wood beams and stud walls. It is more common to find lower to medium finish levels in stick built product.

Podium: This style features a concrete base or "podium" on the first one or two stories with stick built construction on up to five floors over the podium. That base also may include digging down to create a basement or underground parking garage. It is common to find mid to high finish levels in podium product given the higher cost as well as the likelihood that will be developed in an urban location.

Concrete and steel: Urban high-rise buildings that need heavy-duty structural support to accommodate a very dense, vertical format will utilize a combination of concrete and steel. Given the high cost of land, cost of construction and density in this type of location and product, it is most common to find high end finish levels in concrete and steel buildings.

Utilizing the Information

While multifamily real estate has its own unique complexities and risk factors, from an investment and risk analysis perspective, it is generally regarded as the safest of all commercial real estate asset classes (although I know many industrial operators that would challenge that statement). This is predominantly due to higher average occupancies with lower price volatility when compared to other asset classes.

For signs of evidence to support this argument, consider that apartments have a lower cost of capital and wider availability of debt capital. For example, government backed agencies, Fannie Mae and Freddie Mac, will lend on multifamily assets but not on other commercial real estate asset classes. In addition, when looking back at the last recession, generally speaking, multifamily is the asset class that performed the best during the depths of the financial crisis and was the asset class to lead the recovery. There is something to be said for the notion that people still need a place to live no matter the phase of the economic cycle. During recessions, people can lose their homes and be forced into the renter pool,which you as now understand, increases rental demand through a shift in the owner vs. renter household breakout. Once a recovery begins, the shorter lease terms of multifamily allow owners to adjust more quickly to changing market environments.

Investing in Office Real Estate

The U.S. office market traditionally attracts large amounts of investment capital from both institutional and private investors. The sector typically logs well in excess of $100 billion in institutional-quality transactions each year. The National Council of Real Estate Investment Fiduciaries (NCREIF) Index pegs the average annual return for office property over the past 20 years at a healthy 10.3%. In this chapter we provide an overview of the office asset class, highlight key demand drivers including the role of demographics, and conclude with how investors can apply this information to make smarter investment decisions.

The U.S. office market has traditionally attracted large amounts of investment capital from both institutional and private investors. This sector typically logs well in excess of $100 billion in institutional quality transactions each year.

Office is an attractive real estate asset class for a number of reasons. It has strong underlying fundamentals, a diverse base of end users that span a variety of industries, and a long track record of delivering solid returns. On average, the National Council of Real Estate Investment

Fiduciaries (NCREIF) Index tells us that the average annual return for total office property (including income and appreciation) over the past 20 years is a healthy 10.3%. In addition, the office investment sector offers a spectrum of opportunities across the different investment strategies of core, core-plus, value-add and opportunistic – each of which carry inherently different risk-adjusted return scenarios that begin at single digit annualized returns on the conservative end to over 20% annualized returns on opportunistic deals. In this chapter, we will begin with a brief overview of the office asset class, highlight key demand drivers including the role of demographics, and conclude with a discussion on changing uses and how investors can use this information when making investment decisions.

> "Office is the flagship asset class of commercial real estate. In this section, I provide an overview of the asset class, discuss demand drivers and demographics and highlight recent changes in use."
>
> 
> Ian Formigle

Asset Class Overview

Office Buildings are typically defined as having at least 75% of a building's interior space designed and finished as office space. Office buildings are usually split into two categories based on location – central business district (CBD) or suburban. The industry also "grades" properties as Class A, B or C based on criteria such as age, quality, amenities, rent and location among other factors.

CBD vs. Suburban: Throughout the U.S., office markets are generally bifurcated into two subsets a) CBD - the "Central Business District", this is the heart of most office markets and typically possesses the largest concentration of office space and b) Suburban - lower density locations that lie outside of the urban core. Some of the differences to consider when comparing urban versus suburban properties are parking and transit. Urban properties rely more heavily on access to mass transit, while suburban properties require higher parking ratios.

Traditional vs Creative: Traditional office buildings have been the norm in the office world for decades. There is a new and growing segment of the office market that focuses on "creative" space. This sector started gaining a foothold back in the 1980s as older warehouse buildings were repurposed as "trendy" office space with interior design that highlights original brick walls, floors and open ceilings that showed exposed beams and ductwork. It was a favorite among the creative set such as ad agencies and new tech start-ups. The distinction of traditional vs. creative space is intertwined with demographics that are leading to changes in office use; a topic we discuss in greater detail below.

Demand Drivers

It is valuable for office investors to understand the demand drivers that influence occupancies, rental rate growth and new construction. The single largest driver of demand in the office sector is jobs. Traditionally, there has been strong correlation between employment growth and positive absorption of office space. The office sector typically thrives when the economy is growing and companies are expanding, as firms seek more space to accommodate the addition of new workers. Likewise, the office market struggles during periods of flat or declining job growth. In both expanding and contracting markets, the office sector is sensitive to the elastic demand of business and professional services, such as finance, insurance and real estate "FIRE" users as well as information technology employment. Those types of users have appetites for office space that can change rapidly depending on the success or demise of their business models.

There are a wide variety of companies and industries that occupy office space, and those users have vastly different criteria when it comes to choosing space to lease that best fits their needs. For some users, it is all about finding the best location that is close to customers and employees. Other companies are highly sensitive to cost and need to solve to a budget. Others still may prioritize privacy and seek isolated locations with secured access. User requirements can also include a variety of other considerations such as building services and amenities, adequate parking, state-of-the art technology, building infrastructure and the impact of the location on a company's brand identity and image. The key point is that office buildings come in all shapes and sizes. This creates demand for different types of properties and thus different investment opportunities.

Demographics

While some demand drivers such as job growth are difficult to project, demographics are absolute facts. Studying how demographics affect office demand can enable investors to draw asset-based conclusions. Millenials provide an interesting case study in this regard. This demographic will soon represent the largest segment of the workforce. Not surprisingly, their preferences are influencing office location decisions, which has landlords scrambling to better understand them. As a result, modern offices are beginning to look more like professional living rooms rather than the cube farms of decades past.

In addition to a "cool environment" millennials desire a host of on-site or nearby amenities including bike parking, locker rooms and coffee bars as well as other factors such as "green" or energy efficient buildings. If you want to see this vision in action, simply take a tour of the nearest We Work location. This company is evangelical in touting the merits of the modern workplace. Their lobbies feel less like an office building and more like that of a hip hotel. While

We Work's vision may represent one end of the office continuum that is, perhaps, too forward-looking for certain users, companies are increasingly taking cues from this model to seek out amenity rich locations in order to compete for this burgeoning generation of talent.

Changes in Office Use

With a basic grasp of how demographics factor into shifts in office design and use, it becomes easier to contemplate the alternative workplace strategies that are changing how and where people choose to work. While the mass adoption of mobile technologies has certain pundits calling for the end of office space as we know it, a more pragmatic perspective suggests that the way office space is used is changing but that it is still in demand. Working from home or the local coffee shop is not effective for every individual or every business, as the vast majority of workers still need and desire go to an office either part or full-time to do work, collaborate with colleagues and meet with clients. Therefore, demand for office space is not disappearing but evolving.

When considering this evolution, it is important to first consider the factors that affect where companies choose to locate their office. In years past, companies took a car centric approach to office requirements, which translated into demand for suburban business parks with large parking ratios and onsite amenities such as cafeterias. Now, companies increasingly want to be located in vibrant communities surrounded by compelling offsite amenities.

As companies look to answer the question of vibrancy, urbanization trends are influencing location decisions. There is more and more research to support the argument that urban centers are a magnet for commercial and residential development. Those urban hubs often feature a density of different types of real estate uses, including office, residential, retail, restaurants and entertainment. They are highly walkable, as well as linked to mass transit such as high speed bus, subway or light rail systems. All of these aspects provide a compelling argument for why a company should select it for their office location.

But, what may be surprising, is that these urban hubs are not just confined to traditional downtowns, they also are popping up in traditional suburban settings as cities adapt to changing societal demands. We are now seeing the rise of the "Walkable Suburban Village" particularly as certain metros become overly constrained by congestion. In either an urban or suburban location, the common denominator when selecting an office space is that it helps companies to attract and retain talent.

Another consideration in use changes is that certain trends have staying power, while others may be short lived. For example, "open grid" office spaces that features exposed ceilings as part of the décor have been all the rage in the past few years, which sent landlords scrambling to remove ceiling grids and deliver exposed ceiling buildouts to win deals. However, as open grid users have now lived in these environments for a few years now, some are struggling with untenable acoustics, which has led to them to turning away from this design.

CrowdStreet itself is a case study in this phenomenon. Our previous office had an open ceiling complete with exposed ductwork. Initially we were wowed by the creative look but, as our team grew, the acoustics proved overly distracting. When moving to our new location in June, we sought an office environment with an open and collaborative floor plan but one that also offered both carpet and a ceiling grid to help us manage the acoustics. Now a month into our new space, we are highly appreciative of our ceiling grid. While the jury is still out, the staying power of the open ceiling is at least now in question, which argues in favor of maintaining flexibility in the format of an office and not betting the ranch on any single trend.

As investors synthesize asset classes, markets and use types to formulate investment decisions, it is worth keeping in mind that these are the myriad factors that roll up to the overriding consideration, which is relevancy. No matter the type or location of any office asset, the bottom line is that it must be relevant today and maintain its relevancy over the course of the holding period. Understanding classifications, market subtypes, demographics and office uses are all intended to equip you with the knowledge to answer that question. Investors will find a variety of office property offerings, both urban and suburban, on the CrowdStreet Marketplace.

Investing in Hotel Real Estate

Commercial real estate investments are subject to shifts in supply and demand that can have a notable impact on net operating income, profitability and yield. Hospitality is one of the few property types where such shifts are felt almost immediately. However, in exchange for a transient customer base that is not obligated to long term commitments, hotels have the ability to mark rents to market on a daily basis. The upside of this flexibility is that hotels can quickly react to heightened demand and improving economic conditions and raise room rates as much and as fast as the market will bear. In value add scenarios, hotel operators are also able to realize improved asset performance from repositioning efforts or capital improvements more quickly than other asset classes. In this chapter, we provide an asset class overview, explain the key metrics that are used to evaluate hotel performance, highlight recent changes in use and conclude with thoughts on how to use this information to make better informed investment decisions.

Commercial real estate investments are subject to shifts in supply and demand that can have a notable impact on net operating income, profitability and yield. Hospitality is one of the few property types where such shifts are felt almost immediately.

Other asset classes, such as office or retail, utilize medium to long term leases that seek to deliver stable and targetable income streams. Tenants commit to occupy a space and pay a set rate for five, 10 or even 15 years. Even apartment renters sign leases for a year at a time.

Hotels have no such lease agreements. At most, hotel guests may be subject to a non-refundable period as the booking date approaches.

In exchange for a transient customer base that is not obligated to long term commitments, hotels have the ability to mark rents to market on a daily basis. The upside of that flexibility is that hotels can quickly react to heightened demand and improving economic conditions and raise room rates as much and as fast as the market will bear. In value add scenarios, hotel operators are also able to realize improved asset performance from repositioning efforts or capital improvements more quickly than other asset classes. The flip side of this fluidity is that hotels are more susceptible to operating fluctuations when compared to other asset classes.

In this chapter, we will provide an asset class overview, explain the key metrics that are used to evaluate hotel performance, highlight recent changes in use and conclude with thoughts on how to use this information to make informed investment decisions.

Asset Class Overview

Hotels are defined primarily by the services and amenities that they offer. Another key distinction in this category is the "flag" or operating brand that includes the likes of Hilton, Marriott and Holiday Inn among others. The four main types of hotels include:

Full-Service: These hotels are loaded with guest services and amenities, such as on-site restaurants, banquet and meeting rooms, concierge service, spas and retail shops. Some examples include brands such as Hyatt, Ritz-Carlton, St. Regis and Westin. For full service hotels, the overall success of the hotel is highly sensitive to the quality of its onsite amenities, particularly the food and beverage services.

Limited-Service: These properties are a step down in terms of service and amenities but still typically offer meeting rooms, a fitness center and a swimming pool. As a result, the operations of this class of hotel are more predictable in comparison to full-service hotels. Some examples include Courtyard by Marriott, Fairfield Inn, Hampton Inn and Holiday Inn Express.

Budget: These "no frills" hotels may offer one or two guest services or amenities, but they tend to focus on providing the basic necessities for a low rate. Examples include EconoLodge, Super 8 and Starwood's Aloft.

Extended Stay: These hotels are aimed at business travelers on extended assignments, families in the midst of a relocation, and others in need of temporary housing. They offer discounts for stays of five days or greater and provide home-like features that are unavailable at standard hotels, such as self-serve laundry facilities and full kitchens.

There is substantial variation among extended stay hotels with respect to quality and available amenities but most specialize in a mid-range to budget market segments.

Key Metrics

Hotels have unique industry standard metrics to track performance and growth, which include average daily rates (ADR) and revenue per available room (RevPar). These data can be used as benchmarks to gauge performance based on past history as well as compare performance relative to peer hotels that are similar in size, characteristics and location.

> "No other asset class is marked-to-market every day. In this section, I provide an overview of the asset class, discuss industry key metrics as well as demand drivers and recent changes in use."
>
> Ian Formigle

ADR: ADR is the measure of the average rate paid for rooms sold and calculated by dividing room revenue by rooms sold in any given period:

ADR = Room Revenue / Rooms Sold

RevPar: RevPar is the total guest room revenue divided by the total number of available rooms. RevPar is affected by the number of unoccupied available rooms, while ADR shows only the average rate of rooms actually sold.

RevPar = Occupancy Rate x ADR

Example: A hotel has 100 rooms and collected $237,150 in room revenue for the month of January. We also know that this hotel sold 2,325 room nights that month. With this information, we can immediately calculate the hotel's ADR for the month of January:

ADR = $237,150 / 2,325 = $102

Since we know the actual rooms sold in the month of January and the total number of rooms, we also know the occupancy:

Occupancy = rooms sold / total possible rooms sold = 2,325 / (100 rooms x 31 days or 3,100) = 75%

Once we know ADR and occupancy, we can now calculate RevPar:

RevPar = $102 x 75% = $76.50

Knowing only that the hotel's RevPar for January was $76.50 isn't necessarily helpful. However, when we take this information and compare it the RevPar for this same hotel over each of the preceding 12 months as well as compare it to the RevPar of its competitive set for the month of January, we now have a highly useful metric for understanding the performance and competitiveness of this hotel over the defined period.

Demand Drivers

The two core customer groups that fuel demand for hotel rooms are tourism and business travelers. Hotels also have a variety of demand drivers specific to their local market, such as colleges, events and tourist attractions. Tourism tends to drive traffic during weekends or all week during high season periods. Tourism also can be seasonal based on the locale, such as winter ski resorts and fall foliage tours.

Business travel tends to drive occupancy from Sunday through Thursday. Some hotels are better positioned to capture the business traveler, such as with those with on-site meeting and event space. Hotels also can benefit from locations adjacent to or near convention centers. Other hotels are destinations in their own right for business or tourist traffic due to particular locations or amenities, such as casinos or water parks. In addition, hotels can appeal to guests who are seeking out convenience, such as proximity to an airport or a major highway or interstate.

Demand drivers can change as a metro grows. For example, hotels located in CrowdStreet's headquarters of Portland, OR were, as recently as four years ago, plentiful and cheap. But these days, Portland hotel rates have soared in conjunction with the economic and population growth that our city has enjoyed in recent years. Rooms that were previously booked for $150 per night now cost $350 per night or more. Further fueling Portland's hotel demand are a thriving foodie scene and a favorable sales tax environment that attracts luxury goods shoppers. A compelling metro story is one factor in what makes hotel investing attractive, because it is the daily marking to market of rates that allows investors to capitalize on growth as quickly as it materializes.

Changes in Use

The hotel industry has seen substantial change both in terms of how hotels are developed and used as well as how they are marketed. Most changes in use are rooted in the adoption of technology. The following are few of the highlights:

Online Travel Agencies (OTAs): OTAs have had a major impact on how hotels are booked since their inception some twenty years ago. After years of consolidation, the space is now dominated by two players - Expedia and Priceline. OTAs are obviously now pervasive and, as you might expect, have love-hate relationships with hotel operators. On the upside, OTAs drive tremendous traffic to hotels and can readily fill last minute vacancies. The downside of OTAs is that they come with steep commissions that can reach as high as 25% of the booking amount. In addition, the more traffic that flows through OTAs, the more hotels become dependent upon them.

Millennial Hotels: Millennials are driving changes in use of practically everything they touch and hotels are no exception. Through their desire for affordable yet "cool" hotels in urban locations, hotel brands have been rapidly evolving to deliver concepts that cater to their tastes. These hotels feature rooms that are only 1/2 - 2/3 of the size of their traditional competitive set. To generate the space savings, traditional improvements and fixtures such as closets and desks are removed. In exchange for small rooms, these hotels invest heavily into technology and hip, vibrant common areas.

Hotel brands such as Yotel, Marriott's AC and Moxy Hotel and Commune's Tommie brands have emerged in this new hotel segment. On the affordable end of the spectrum, Starwood's Aloft Hotels target the Millennial demographic. Even Sir Richard Branson is getting in the mix with a new millennial-oriented chain, dubbed Virgin Hotels. While some pundits argue that the Millennial hotel is a fad, it is nonetheless changing the industry landscape and bringing a new breed of hotel to a magnitude of urban destinations.

Use periods: Another way in which technology is changing the use of hotels is by enabling guests to redefine the period of the traditional night stay. Microbooking apps such as HotelsByDay, Recharge and DayUse allow guests to book hotels by the hour and, in some cases, even by the minute. These apps are yet another example of how technology can be used to generate efficiencies - in this case to fill intraday hotel vacancies that would otherwise go unused.

Synthesizing the Information

Anyone who has traveled for either business or pleasure can grasp the basic building blocks of a successful hotel investment, which include: product offering, service, location, and competitiveness.

It also doesn't require an industry veteran to appreciate that investing in a five-star hotel doesn't necessarily correlate to earning five-star returns. When you stand in the lobby of a five-star hotel and see the huge staff counts and lavish surroundings and then compare that hotel to a limited-service hotel with a small staff that operate in an functional yet cost efficient environment, it wouldn't shock you to learn that the limited-service hotel may actually be more profitable on a per room basis.

The takeaway is that hotels across all categories and price points have their own market segments, competitive sets and corresponding metrics. The key is to conduct a comparative analysis amongst similar hotels in order to determine whether or not the subject asset stands to win greater than, equal to or less than its fair share of its market demand. Much of that analysis is a logical application of things that, from the perspective of a guest, provide a compelling hotel experience. After all, if you love it then others will too and they will be willing to pay up for the experience. If you pair a compelling experience with an efficient cost structure, you have a winner.

There are a variety of entry points into hospitality real estate investments with a host of strategies. If you would like to learn about other asset classes, please check out our chapter, "The Definitive Guide to Real Estate Property Types".

Investing in Industrial Real Estate

The industrial sector is arguably the least glamorous commercial real estate asset class. Over the long run, industrial properties are steady performers, which is why they merit inclusion in real estate investment portfolios. The average annual total return for industrial properties over the past 20 years is 10.6%, which is slightly ahead of the average return of 10.2% across all property types, according to the National Council of Real Estate Investment Fiduciaries (NCREIF) Index. In this chapter, we begin with an overview of the industrial asset class, discuss demand drivers as well as changes in use and conclude with thoughts on how to use this information in making informed investment decisions.

The industrial sector is arguably the least glamorous commercial real estate asset class. There are no elaborate architectural design features, resort-like amenities or high-profile addresses. Instead, industrial real estate is intended to provide practical and efficient space to users that prioritize function over form. Industrial buildings are suitable for a variety of uses such as manufacturing, R&D and the storage and distribution of goods.

Over the long run, industrial properties are steady performers, which is why they merit inclusion in real estate investment portfolios. The average annual total return for industrial properties over the past 20 years is 10.6%, which is slightly ahead of the average return of 10.2% across all property types, according to the National Council of Real Estate Investment Fiduciaries (NCREIF) Index.

In this chapter, we begin with an overview of the industrial asset class, discuss demand drivers as well as changes in use and conclude with thoughts on how to use this information in making informed investment decisions.

Asset Class Overview

The three main categories of industrial real estate are manufacturing, warehouse and Flex/R&D, which are defined as follows by the National Association of Industrial & Office Parks (NAIOP):

Manufacturing: A facility used for the conversion, fabrication and/or assembly of raw or partly wrought materials into products/goods. These properties tend to have less than 20% office space and can be further classified for a heavy or light industrial use.

Warehouse: A facility primarily used for the storage and/or distribution of materials, goods and merchandise. These buildings tend to have less than 15% office space, and modern facilities have high clear ceiling heights that allow for more cubic storage space. This category also may include specialty facilities, such as cold or freezer storage for food.

Flex/R&D: These industrial buildings are designed to give its occupants flexibility in use of the space. Sometimes referred to as flex/tech space, these buildings are an office-industrial hybrid that can have 30% to even 100% office finish.

Because they require a lot of acreage for wide building footprints, low-density parking, and truck turning, industrial buildings are almost never found in the CBD. Therefore, it is rare to hear them distinguished according to anything other than use.

Demand Drivers

There are a number of factors to consider when analyzing industrial investment opportunities.

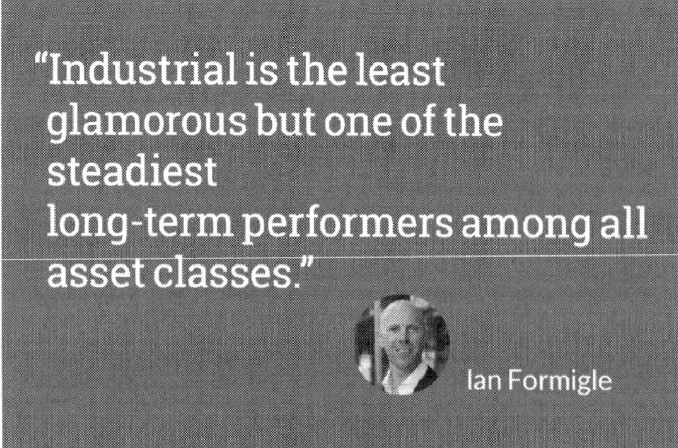

Chief among those factors are location, proximity to customers and workers, transportation, access to land and financial incentives that can offset building costs.

Transportation: Industrial real estate depends on easy access to major highways and interstates; intermodal rail; ports; and air freight and, as a result, serves as a significant driver for industrial demand. Louisville, for example, is home to a major shipping hub for UPS, which has helped to attract dozens of e-commerce and retail firms such as Amazon, Columbia and Guess, as well as manufacturers such as GE.

E-commerce: E-commerce acts as a substantial demand driver for industrial real estate, particularly in larger format buildings. For example, according to Costar, since 2010, one-third of all industrial leases over 500,000 square feet have been for e-commerce purposes. As for market size, Forrester Research projects that U.S. e-commerce sales will surpass $400 billion by 2018. Correspondingly, the demand drivers of e-commerce are omnipresent and only gaining momentum.

Incentives: Locating large industrial facilities often involves working closely with local city or state agencies to negotiate incentives that can influence location decisions. Large industrial properties such as a manufacturing plant, distribution center or data center can have a big tax benefit, and cities and states compete aggressively for bigger projects that will boost their tax base with jobs and property taxes. Those bidding wars include offers of tax rebates, low-cost loans and even free land that can have a big impact on a project's overall cost and ROI for investors.

Changes in Industrial Use

The use of industrial real estate has evolved substantially over the last twenty years. The following are just a few highlights of how uses have changed.

Early Suppression Fast Response ("ESFR") Fire Sprinkler Systems: For warehouse users, fire protection is a major issue, considering that warehouse fires are difficult to suppress and can be devastatingly costly. In years past, a common practice was to augment standard sprinkler systems with an additional "in-rack" system that snakes sprinkler heads through the warehouse rack system. As you might imagine, in-rack systems are costly to install, prohibit further alteration of the warehouse rack system after installation and are prone to operational issues.

The drawbacks of in-rack sprinkler systems have led to the rise of ESFR sprinkler systems. ESFR sprinklers detect and respond to fire much faster than a conventional sprinkler head and spray far greater quantities of water. For example, while a conventional sprinkler head outputs 25 to 30 gallons per minute, an ESFR sprinkler head can output up to 100 gallons per minute. These performance differences enable industrial users to obtain the same or greater level of fire suppression of the in-rack system while foregoing the high cost of installation and ongoing headaches of operation.

Taller Clear Heights: Over the last 30 years, industrial buildings have grown taller to address demand for increased warehouse efficiency. As recently as the 1970s, most buildings were built with clear heights below 20 feet. As modern warehousing practices spread throughout the country, many tenants demanded more "cubic" space in their facilities, which led to the construction of buildings with 24-, 28-, 32- and now even 36 foot clear heights.

A building's clear height is defined as the usable height to which a tenant can store its product on racking. While the height of a pallet of goods varies, the most common pallet size is 64 inches, estimated to be used approximately 50 percent of the time. That means 32-foot clear facilities can rack between four and six pallets. By jumping up to a 36-foot clear height building, a user will usually be able to rack one pallet position higher, which increases capacity by 10 to 25 percent with the same footprint.

While more efficient, the cost of developing a building to the 36-foot clear height is much than lower clear height buildings. The net result is that 32- and 36-foot clear height buildings are the new class of A buildings, while 20- to 24- foot clear height buildings are usually now considered Class B (for more information on asset classes please see our chapter "Making the Grade in Real Estate: Understanding Class A, B and C") . It is important to note that many warehouse tenants do not require 32- or 36-foot clear heights, which enables them to lease highly functional Class B space at a substantial discount to Class A building rents.

Distribution vs. Fulfillment: Logistics is becoming an increasingly important factor in the use of industrial real estate. Traditionally, distribution involves the storage and shipment of goods to stores in large batches. Fulfillment is a fundamentally different type of use that involves the shipment of products to consumers in small batches. Distribution can function in semi-rural locations where land is cheap and plentiful. Fulfillment, however, requires proximity to major MSAs and/or transportation hubs to facilitate fast deliveries to end users.

The shift in consumer behavior due to e-commerce is changing the use of certain types of industrial real estate as fulfillment has different locational requirements and functional needs such as greater parking ratios. Particularly, as e-commerce retailers are racing for the prize of same day delivery, the fulfillment center is emerging as its own subset of industrial use.

Synthesizing the Information

Assembling the above information into a useful set of tools to evaluate potential industrial investment opportunities boils down to relevancy. When thinking through industrial real estate, it's helpful to take a macro to micro approach. First, consider what is happening at the metro level in terms of how it uses industrial real estate, which metros are offering incentives to developers and how market demands are changing uses within those metros. From there, look to the submarkets within the metro that possess the best access to key modes of transportation as it is those markets that will attract the most tenants. Finally, when drilling down to the asset level, consider the asset's ability to serve the needs of the modern industrial tenant. As we mentioned at the outset, those needs are almost purely functional, so the asset needn't be pretty. Instead, a viable asset offers things such as competent fire suppression, adequate clear heights for its intended use and good ingress and egress. While not perfect, if you can gain comfort at each level as you conduct a macro to micro analysis, you likely have a winner.

Investing in Senior Housing Real Estate

Senior housing is a niche property type that has moved into the mainstream of commercial real estate investing in recent years. Both institutional and private investors have been expanding into senior housing, in large part due to the powerful demographic trend of an aging baby boomer population. In addition, the recent economic recession provided further evidence that senior housing tends to be a more resilient real estate property type that doesn't experience the same level of occupancy swings as other asset classes during economic downturns. In this chapter, we will provide an asset class overview, highlight recent changes in use and conclude with thoughts on how investors can use this information to make informed investment decisions.

Senior housing is a niche property type that has moved into the mainstream of commercial real estate investing in recent years. Both institutional and private investors have been expanding into senior housing for a variety of reasons. Chief among them is the powerful demographic trend of an aging baby boomer population.

In addition, the recent economic recession provided further evidence that senior housing tends to be a more resilient real estate property type that doesn't experience the same level of occupancy swings as other asset classes during economic downturns. Heated competition in traditional multifamily assets also has benefited senior housing as some investors have branched out into alternative housing investments.

Combined, all of these factors are fueling investor demand. The total size of the senior housing and care investment property market is estimated to be between $250 billion and $270 billion, according to the National Investment Center for the Seniors Housing & Care Industry (NIC). The non-profit group also estimates that the senior housing market in the U.S. encompasses roughly 22,000 properties and 2.9 million units/beds, including those market rate properties with at least 25 units/beds.

In this chapter, we will provide an asset class overview, highlight recent changes in use and conclude with thoughts on how investors can use this information to make informed investment decisions.

Asset Class Overview

Senior housing properties aim to provide both housing and services to seniors. The three main categories of senior housing include independent living, assisted living and skilled nursing facilities. Memory care is another specialized type of care that may be included as its own separate category or as a subset within assisted living. The NIC provides a detailed description of the different property types, as well as a variety of research and resources for investors, owners and operators.

Independent Living: Designed for senior who require little or no assistance. These properties often cater to residents who are 55+ with a variety of on-site amenities and social programming. Fine dining services may be offered with custom-designed meal packages. These properties generally cater to healthy, active senior with an emphasis on hospitality-style services and features. A variety of apartment sizes are available from studios to large two bedrooms.

Assisted Living: These licensed facilities combine housing with a variety of personal support services and health-care assistance. Residents are not fully independent, and either want or need extra services related to medical care, or help with everyday needs such as transportation, meals and laundry.

Memory care: These long-term care properties serve residents with memory impairment, primarily dementia and Alzheimer's, that makes it unsafe for them to continue to live at home or with a family member. Also called special care units (SCUs), memory care properties often provide 24-hour supervised care within a separate wing or floor of an assisted living facility.

"The demographic trends for senior housing are compelling. In this section, I provide an overview of the asset class, discuss demand drivers and highlight recent changes in use."

Ian Formigle

Skilled Nursing: Properties are generally licensed and provide 24-hour skilled care for chronic and short-term conditions that require more intensive or specialized medical and nursing care. Memory Care Rehab centers are another subset within this category that provide healthcare services to both senior and non-senior who are in need of a high level of care on a short-term basis, such as during recovery from a major surgery or injury.

Campuses: Senior properties can be configured as stand-alone or adjoining facilities, as well as campus-style continuing care retirement communities (CCRCs). CCRCs offer a tiered approach to the aging process as they allow residents to move from one type of facility to another in the same location as their level of care needs change. Those campuses also are ideal for spouses or siblings who want to live close together but have different care needs.

Demand Drivers

The demand for senior housing is influenced by two key factors. One is needs based. Some seniors have a need for assistance as they age. That demand for personal and healthcare-related services drives demand for assisted living, memory care and nursing care. A second factor is simple lifestyle choice. Some seniors choose to live in 55+ communities for the social benefits of living near their peers, as well as more convenience and lower maintenance associated with an apartment versus a home and amenities such as meal plans. Based on 2010 population estimates, over 20% of the 12 million households headed by persons at least 75 years old reside in senior housing and care properties, according to the NIC.

Demographics: One of the factors that has attracted capital to the senior housing sector is its favorable demographics. As of 2016, 15% of the U.S. population (49 million people) was age 65 or older, and by 2030, 21% of the population (74 million people) will be 65+. Those boomers are having both a direct and indirect impact on senior housing properties. Baby boomers are actively moving into 55+ independent living properties. However, the typical age for seniors entering assisted living facilities these days is 80, and the first baby boomers do not turn 80 until 2026. Therefore, boomers won't have a significant direct impact on demand for assisted living and skilled nursing facilities for another decade. Boomers are a big influencer of demand for assisted living and skilled nursing facilities as they are the children of today's residents.

Memory care: Baby boomers also will drive demand for more specialized memory care facilities, which can affect seniors at earlier ages than other aging needs. Of the 5.4 million Americans with Alzheimer's, an estimated 5.2 million people are age 65 and older, and approximately 200,000 individuals are under age 65 with younger-onset Alzheimer's, according to the Alzheimer's Association. Unless there is a medical breakthrough, the number of people age 65 and older with Alzheimer's disease could nearly triple to a projected 13.8 million by 2050.

Geographic concentration: The demand for senior housing properties is widespread across the country from major metros to very small tertiary markets. However, a large population base – and especially a concentration of aging seniors – will drive more demand for senior housing properties.

Notably, there is a greater concentration of senior living in three key states – California, Florida and New York.

Changes in Use

Across all types of senior housing, one of the most notable changes over the past two decades has been a continual shift away from institutional style facilities. Residents – and their children who are making those housing decisions – have higher expectations for care, which has influenced the level of services delivered by senior housing operators as well as the quality of the physical environment. As such, all types of senior housing properties are finding that they have to step-up their game in order to compete for residents.

Upgrading image: Developers are thinking strategically about their customer base, as well as the decision makers for those customers. For example, what locations are most convenient for those children to stop and visit mom or dad, and what types of facilities do they want to choose for their parents? What was acceptable in the 1980s is not acceptable today. Facilities are aimed at keeping seniors happy and engaged, giving them a better quality of life and also prolonging their life. Today's properties offer a variety of on-site amenities, such as nail salons, nature trails and chef-run restaurants.

Thoughtful design: Facility designs are being re-engineered with more inviting atmospheres that are both appealing and therapeutic to residents. For example, select memory care facilities are incorporating retro environments, such as a 1950's soda fountain. Studies have shown that seniors who suffer from dementia are stimulated by these simulated environments and begin to behave more like the youthful version of themselves that coincide with the period of the environment. Operators are also infusing biophilic designs and introducing natural elements, such as living plant walls and raw-edged wooden tables to add warmth to a space by bringing nature indoors. Incorporating nature in this way has shown to positively affect those in the space by reducing stress and improving cognitive performance, emotions and mood.

Emphasis on Wellness: The concept of preventative care has finally made its way into the operational of modern senior housing facilities. Many communities are choosing to add resort-caliber spas and fitness rooms, residents are seeking and able to utilize such amenities.

Technology: One of the most prolific changes in senior housing facilities is the adoption of technology. Tech implementation begins with simple items such as Wifi to Wii games that can help keep residents engaged and active. State-of-the-art tech also is increasingly used to monitor residents for health and safety purposes and substantiate the level of care residents are receiving for their family members. For example, caregivers in modern facilities are now often equipped with smart phone apps to log and input data live during resident visits rather than relying on outmoded documentation procedures. In addition, surveillance systems such as live webcams enable the children of residents to log into secure portals and "virtually" check in on their parent.

Synthesizing the Information

Senior housing has some distinct differences compared to other real estate property types. For starters, it is one of three asset classes (the other two being hotels and self-storage) that are essentially operating businesses attached to real estate. For this reason, investors should investigate the manager or operator just as stringently as the fundamentals of the underlying real estate when contemplating a senior housing investment. By analyzing a deal against the backdrop of local demographics and with attention to items such as modern design and a progressive operating strategy, investors can gain better insight into the probability of a particular investment meeting or exceeding its targeted goals.

Second, there are different payment options that include private pay (residents paying out-of-pocket), and/or payment through other means such as long-term care insurance, Medicare, Medicaid or veteran's benefits. Some of the public programs can be more sensitive to limits on reimbursement or legislation that may affect billing processes and payments. Therefore, properties whose business models are oriented predominantly or exclusively towards private pay are far less vulnerable to payment terms risk and bureaucratic complexities.

For investors, identifying a competitive senior housing investment offering begins by confirming the following attributes:

- A primary market with robust demand
- An experienced and sophisticated operator
- An operating strategy that possesses a modern approach; and
- An appealing facility that will attract residents

If those four key elements are in place, then investors, subject to review of supporting materials, are likely on their way to identifying a competitive property.

Investing in Self-Storage Real Estate

Self-storage is a unique asset class. It has a reputation of providing relatively high yields and has also been potentially resistant to recessions due to its lower declines and default ratios vis-à-vis other asset classes. Based on our research, publicly traded self-storage REITs have been one of the top performing sectors in recent years with a good track record of delivering potential dividends and stock appreciation. In fact, our research indicates that the industry has been considered by Wall Street analysts to be "recession resistant" based on its performance during the last economic recession. In this chapter, we provide an asset class overview, highlight recent changes in use and conclude with thoughts on how to use this information to make informed self-storage investment decisions.

Self-storage is a unique asset class. It has a reputation of providing relatively high yields and has also been potentially to be resistant to recessions due to its lower declines and default ratios vis-à-vis other asset classes. While still a relatively new industry that really got its start in the 1960's, self-storage is already sizable. According to the research group, IBISWorld, there are over 54,000 storage facilities across the U.S. with 2014 - 2016 estimated revenues as follows:

2014 (estimate): $29.8 billion

2015 (estimate): $31.6 billion

2016 (forecast): $32.7 billion

Self-storage falls into one of three asset classes (the other two being hotels and senior housing) that are essentially operating businesses attached to real estate. This obviously places more emphasis on the skills of the operator and, in the case of self-storage, it has translated into substantial room for improvement in operational efficiencies. In its early years, the industry was largely dominated by mom-and-pop operators and, even today, is still highly fragmented. As self-storage gained traction, large branded chains such as Public Storage, CubeSmart and StorQuest, entered the market and elevated business practices, quality of real estate and operating efficiency.

Today self-storage is less of the well-kept secret it once was due to growing institutional ownership and public reporting requirements of those entities. Based on our research publicly traded self-storage REITs have been one of the top performing sectors in recent years with a good track record of delivering dividends and stock appreciation. In fact, our research indicates that the industry has been considered by Wall Street analysts to be "recession resistant" based on its performance during the last economic recession.

In this chapter, we will provide an asset class overview, highlight recent changes in use, discuss low-minimum options for investing in self-storage, and conclude with thoughts on how investors can use this information to make informed investment decisions.

Asset Class Overview

Self-storage facilities vary in size, quality and construction. Some properties have been designed and built specifically for self-storage, while others have been converted from a prior use such as a warehouse, car dealership or vacant big box retail. Properties can be one-story with drive-up access as well as multi-story that offer access via elevators and internal hallways. Storage properties rent units, often in different size configurations, on a month-to-month or short-term basis.

> "Self-storage is a relatively new asset class for which demand has continually surged since it debut in the 1960's. In this section, I provide an overview of the asset class, discuss demand drivers and highlight recent changes in use."
>
> 
> Ian Formigle

Drive Up / Outdoor Bay: The first generation of self-storage projects were almost exclusively this type, which feature rows of storage buildings with outdoor roll up doors that are accessed by vehicle. They offer minimal security other than padlocks and on-premises video cameras, and are always one story in height. In exchange, they are typically the least expensive to rent.

Climate-controlled: Facilities that offer climate controlled and humidity controlled space in all or part of properties have become increasingly popular over the past decade. People don't want to store items only to return to clothing or furniture that is musty and moldy or documents that have been destroyed by mildew, and they are willing to pay a premium to protect their belongings.

Specialty storage: Properties can cater to specialty storage needs within all or part of a facility, such as boats, cars, documents, wine and art.

Mixed-use: Storage-facilities may boost income by incorporating a variety of other uses, such as adding retail or office space for lease. Properties also may operate complementary businesses at the same property, such as truck-rentals or a pack-and-ship franchise.

Demand Drivers

Population growth: Self-storage facilities are a destination property, meaning that it is not an impulse stop where facilities need a high-profile location. However, customers also like convenience. Since population growth is a logical driver of storage demand, self-storage developers are looking at real estate more strategically and locating closer to their customer bases as they try to outmaneuver their competition. Storage does well in densely populated areas, as well as markets that are experiencing population and job growth.

American consumerism: People buy a lot of stuff and have a natural reluctance to throw anything out. Suburban garages fill up quickly with a variety of memorabilia and toys from skateboards and skis to boats and snowmobiles.

Transition: Self-storage gets an added boost in demand from people who are in transition that may need a temporary or even longer term storage alternative. For example, self-storage partially benefitted from the recession as people that were displaced from their homes or relocated to new jobs created demand for storage. Many storage facilities target locations near apartment properties where there tends to be a bigger need for storage and a constant ebb and flow of people. College students and members of the military are both attractive target demographics.

Changes in Use

The self storage industry has seen substantial change both in terms of how locations are developed and used as well as how they are operated. The following are few of the highlights:

Location: In the past, self-storage properties were located on the periphery of a metro or tucked away in the back of an industrial park. Over the past decade, self-storage properties have moved into urban centers to be closer to their customers. That shift has been propelled by the new trend of urbanization as demographics such as Millennials and Empty Nesters are moving to cities only to find that their new urban dwellings fail to offer sufficient space to store their gear. Storage facilities are following the rooftops.

Design: Competition is one of the drivers that have helped to elevate design standards. As storage operators have pushed harder for retail locations that get them closer to customers, they are finding that they have to upgrade their image to both attract customers and satisfy city building and zoning requirements in those retail locations. In essence, the "no frills" storage properties of the past are being replaced with a new generation of facilities that emphasize upscale designs and even landscaping that position themselves as a more retail-friendly type of use rather than a property that needs to be hidden away in an industrial park or outlying rural area.

Technology: Operators are embracing technology in all aspects of their business. There is growing competitive pressure to offer facilities that are clean, safe and secure. In response to market demands, facilities are incorporating technology into surveillance and security ranging from CCTV monitoring to key card access. Operators also are utilizing technology to improve efficiencies, such as using software to track renter history and issue alerts to late payers or send automatic notifications for rent increases.

Synthesizing the Information

As a recent Forbes article "How Humdrum Self-Storage Became The Hottest Way To Invest In Real Estate" discussed, investors are recognizing self-storage as a potentially lucrative property type known for generating solid and stable cash-on-cash returns with a lean operating strategy. Once someone rents a unit and moves in their items, they don't visit it every day, which translates into a lower need to hire a lot of staff to manage properties.

Self-storage also has lower costs associated with tenant turnover as there are no costly broker fees or tenant improvement dollars necessary to market units to new users. Also, the immediate reusability of a storage space is unmatched amongst other asset classes. Even industrial users often negotiate small upgrades such as refreshed bathrooms or improved loading when signing leases, which can both slow the time to re-lease as well as increase turn costs.

While relatively simplistic in comparison to other asset classes, one factor for investors to take into account when weighing self-storage investment opportunities is that new, modern facilities have become far more expensive to build than the previous generation of facilities. Land costs alone in urban areas can be as much as 50 percent of a total project cost, according to the Self Storage Association. That higher cost is important to consider when assessing opportunities to invest in new developments. Will a project be able to charge high enough rents to justify the construction costs? Or when buying an existing property, a higher price may be warranted because the construction costs create a barrier to entry for competition entering the market. The bottom line is that the industry is evolving rapidly so you can't use a decade old method of analysis when looking at the current competitive landscape.

One mitigating factor to rental rate risk is that the self storage facilities typically rely upon lower occupancy levels in comparison to other asset classes. For example, the breakeven occupancy rate to service normal debt amounts for a self storage facility is usually 40% to 45% as compared to 65% or more for apartments, retail and office. Consequently, once delivered and stabilized, self storage facilities tend to hold value better and recover faster than other assets when real estate markets sour. According to data reported by NAREIT, self storage had the highest total annual returns over 5-, 10-, and 15-year averages in an analysis of five different property sectors from 1994 to 2011.

When you put it all together, an asset class that is known to be recession resistant yet offer stable cash flow and, at a macro level, is characterized as a growing yet consolidating market, poses a relatively compelling argument for inclusion in a diversified commercial real estate portfolio.

CRE Metrics & Definitions

Understanding Internal Rate of Return (IRR) in Real Estate Investing

The Internal Rate of Return (IRR) is the metric most commonly used to measure profitability of a potential real estate investment. In this chapter, we define the IRR and describe its strengths and weaknesses.

The IRR is defined as the discount rate at which the net present value of a set of cash flows (ie, the initial investment, expressed negatively, and the returns, expressed positively) equals zero. In more simple terms, it is the rate at which a real estate investment grows (or, heaven forbid, shrinks). In this sense, you can think of it as a time sensitive compounded annual rate of return.

The IRR is useful because it can provide an "apples-to-apples" comparison of two cash flows with different distribution timing. To help illustrate the concept, consider the following three examples.

Example 1 - The Coupon

The first example is a typical debt investment with regular distributions and no upside or downside participation and no fee upon sale. In this example, the investment is in a stabilized property that receives 10% annual distributions until the return of capital at the end of year 5 after sale of the property.

		Year 1	Year 2	Year 3	Year 4	Year 5
Initial Investment	($10,000)					
Operation Cash Flow		$1,000	$1,000	$1,000	$1,000	$1,000
Return of Capital						$10,000
SUM	($10,000)	$1,000	$1,000	$1,000	$1,000	$11,000
IRR	10%					

This sort of regular payment schedule is sometimes referred to as a coupon because of its regularity (bonds used to have physical, detachable coupons which investors would redeem), and in this case it is the same as the IRR - 10%. The investment grows by 10% per year evenly.

Example 2 - The Annual Pref with Upside

In the second example, we add in some upside on sale. In this case, the operational cash flows are still regular, allowing for 8% annual distributions; however, there is participation in the profits from sale in year 5.

		Year 1	Year 2	Year 3	Year 4	Year 5
Initial Investment	($10,000)					
Operation Cash Flow		$800	$800	$800	$800	$800
Sale Profit						$1,220
Return of Capital						$10,000
SUM	($10,000)	$800	$800	$800	$800	$12,020
IRR	10%					

Here, the IRR is the same as the first example - 10%. Despite receiving less cash during the first four years, the two investments accumulate returns over the 5-year term at the same rate. Notice that it takes more cash to achieve the same IRR. This is because of the time value of money.

Example 3 - The Value-Add

In this final example, we replace the 8% annual distributions with irregular payments. Suppose the business plan is to renovate and re-tenant an office building. In the first year there is no operating income, and in years 2 and 3 half of the operating income is held in reserve for tenant improvements as the lease up occurs. The building reaches stabilization in year 4 and is sold in year 5. The distributions look like this:

		Year 1	Year 2	Year 3	Year 4	Year 5
Initial Investment	($10,000)					
Operation Cash Flow		$0	$400	$400	$800	$800
Sale Profit						$3,410
Return of Capital						$10,000
SUM	($10,000)	$0	$400	$400	$800	$14,210
IRR	10%					

Again, the IRR is the same as the first two examples - 10%. Again, the investment accumulates wealth for the investor at the same rate over the same time period despite having zero income in the first year and less income in years 2 and 3.

A real estate investor presented with only the IRR, without knowing anything else about distribution schedule or business plan, would not be able to conclude which deal is best suited for his/her investment criteria. One of the keys to IRR analysis, though, is realizing that timing plays an important role. The time or duration of the investment hold period and the timing that cash distributions are paid to investors both have a big influence on this equation.

When bigger isn't always better

It is often assumed that bigger is better – a 15% IRR is more attractive than a 10% IRR. However, one of the problems with using an IRR analysis is that it can be misleading if used alone. How an investor reaches that IRR also can be an important factor to consider when comparing real estate investment opportunities. While a bigger IRR might look good at face value, it is important for investors to look below the surface to see the terms and assumptions used to derive the IRR as well as also consider desire for operational distributions. That is why investors often use IRR in conjunction with other metrics when analyzing the merits of a particular real estate investment offering. In our next chapter, we show how investors can quickly learn a lot about an investment simply by comparing the IRR to the average cash-on-cash return and the equity multiple.

A note on CrowdStreet's standards

As we've seen, there are ways to manipulate the IRR based on how you calculate targeted returns. For instance, a sponsor might present a project-level IRR; however, this rate of return is not an apples-to-apples comparison with a net-to-investor IRR because it does not take into account sponsor fees and promotes. In the cases where there are fees or promotes, the project-level IRR will be greater than the net-to-investor IRR, meaning the investor stands to receive less than what the project-level IRR might seem to represent. On the CrowdStreet Marketplace, all IRR targets are net-to-investor unless explicitly stated otherwise.

> "IRR is the most commonly used metric when calculating real estate returns. In this section, I describe how to calculate IRRs and outline the pros and cons of using an IRR to assess returns."
>
> 
> Ian Formigle

Also, it has become fairly standard in the industry to calculate the IRR on an investment based on an annualized roll-up of what might actually be monthly or quarterly distributions. Namely, the calculation assumes that cash flow is distributed once per year. This is done to make the presentation of material simpler, avoid confusion about how the IRR is calculated for any given deal and provide the most conservative interpretation of a series of annual targeted cash flows. Given the time sensitivity of the IRR, increasing the frequency of the distributions in the calculation (to quarterly or monthly) will increase the number and, actually, change it to a different formula known as an XIRR. This is one of the industry tricks that, when abused, can sometimes be labeled as "financial engineering". The point is that when comparing IRRs across multiple deals, be sure to check the type of IRR calculation for each deal to avoid falling prey to this potential trap. On the CrowdStreet Marketplace, all IRR projections are calculated on an annualized basis unless explicitly stated otherwise.

What is a Cash-on-Cash Return?

A common metric for measuring commercial real estate investment performance is the cash-on-cash return, which is sometimes also referred to as the cash yield. The cash-on-cash return rate can provide useful insight into the business plan for a property and the likelihood of receiving regular cash distributions over the course of an investment.

A common metric for measuring commercial real estate investment performance is the cash-on-cash return, which is sometimes also referred to as the cash yield. It is a fairly simple calculation that is reached by dividing the annual pre-tax cash flow by the total cash invested. For example, if an investor puts $100,000 cash into the purchase of an apartment building and the annual pre-tax cash flow they receive is $10,000, then their cash-on-cash return is 10%.

Cash-on-cash return = annual pre-tax cash flow / total cash invested

The cash-on-cash return is typically a measure of operational cash flow and, therefore, excludes any profits realized from a capital event such as sale or refinance.

Although the cash-on-cash return may help to quantify cash distributions, one key point that investors need to recognize is that any forward-looking cash-on-cash return is not promised but targeted. In other words, it is not an obligation. In this way, the cash-on-cash return is different from a coupon or debt payment, which is a regularly scheduled payment that an operator must meet, despite changes in the business plan or eventualities. As a result, investors should be cautious to equate a targeted cash-on-cash return to a debt coupon. The actual cash-on-cash return may be higher or lower than the targeted number.

> "This metric is commonly used in commercial real estate to calculate annual yield. In this section, I define cash-on-cash returns and highlight how they are often misinterpreted as distribution yields."
>
> Ian Formigle

Even though it is a targeted metric, the cash-on-cash return is the most useful metric to estimate the distributions that an investor might receive over the course of the investment period. The cash-on-cash return is also distinct from the preferred return, which is an annual return priority that may or may not be paid current and may not reflect the actual cash to be paid out in any given year.

The cash-on-cash return rate can provide useful insight into the business plan for a property and the likelihood of receiving regular cash distributions over the course of an investment.

What is a Preferred Return?

A common feature of a real estate equity waterfall, the preferred return or "pref" can be particularly tricky for investors who are not familiar with its permutations. Not all prefs are calculated in the same way. In this chapter, we explain the different types of prefs and walk you through several examples to distinguish these prefs from other frequently conflated topics such as the "preferred equity" or "pref equity" position in the capital stack.

A common feature of a real estate equity waterfall, the "preferred return" or "pref" can be particularly tricky for investors who are not familiar with its permutations. Not all prefs are calculated in the same way. In this chapter, we explain the different types of prefs and distinguish these prefs from the "preferred equity" or "pref equity" position in the capital stack.

What is a preferred return?

As the name suggests, preferred return is a profit distribution preference whereby profits, either from operations, sale, or refinance, are distributed to one class of equity before another until a certain rate of return on the initial investment is reached. The pref is stated as a percentage, such as an 8% cumulative return on initial investment; however it can also be stated as a certain equity multiple. This preference provides some comfort to investors since it subordinates the sponsor's profits participation or "promote" (see our chapter: What is a Real Estate Sponsor Promote?) up to a certain return threshold.

Preferred Return v. Preferred Equity

The preferred return is distinct from the idea of "preferred equity," which is a position in the capital stack that has a repayment priority. The difference lies in the return on and return of capital. The preferred return is a preference in the returns on capital, while a preferred equity position is one that receives a preference in the return of capital. In most true preferred equity investments, investors get their initial investment and also get a set percentage return on their investment before the subordinate equity investor gets even $1 dollar of cash flow. If the investor does not receive a return of capital before the sponsor or some other equity tranche, then the investor is in a "common" or "JV equity" position and not a preferred equity position.

For further discussion of priorities in return of capital, please check out our capital stack chapter.

The True v. Pari Passu Preferred Return

"The preferred return is a tricky metric because it can be confused with preferred equity. In this section, I define the preferred return and describe how it differs when used in a common equity and preferred equity positions."

Ian Formigle

An investor in a common equity position can still receive a pref, and the type of pref can be further distinguished based on the treatment of sponsor capital, called the co-investment. If the investor receives a preferred return (i.e. profits) before a sponsor does, then the pref is a "true" preferred return; however, if the investor and the sponsor receive the same preferred return, paid at the same time, the pref is a "pari-passu preferred return." With a true pref, the investor receives preferential treatment on its capital contribution; with a pari-passu pref, the investor does not.

Instead, the pari-passu pref acts as a threshold up to which investor and sponsor capital are treated equally and over which the sponsor capital receives a promote.

To help clarify these concepts, consider the following examples. The returns in these examples are not necessarily indicative of prevailing market rates.

Preferred Equity

Capital Contribution:	
Sponsor	10%
Investors	90%
Distribution Priority:	
First	To investors until they reach an 10% annualized return

Second	Return of investor capital
Third	20% to investors and 80% to sponsor

In this example of preferred equity, the investors first receive their capital contributions plus a 10% annualized return before the sponsor receives any money. Second, the sponsor receives its capital contribution. Finally, investors receive 20% of all excess profits with the sponsor receiving 80% of all excess profits. The investors receive a true preferred return rate and, in exchange, they receive only 20% of profits over their 10% true preferred return. Overall, the return is likely to be lower than if they participated in the upside in a JV equity position; however, their overall investment risk is lower.

Common Equity with a True Pref

Capital Contribution:	
Sponsor	10%
Investors	90%
Distribution Priority:	
First	To investors until they reach an 6% annualized return
Second	Investor and sponsor return of capital pro rata
Third	60% to investors and 40% to sponsor

In this example of a common equity investment with a true pref, the investors receive a 6% annualized return before then sponsor receives any money. The difference is that the sponsor receives a return of capital pro rata with the investors. Above the 6% investor pref, investors and sponsor divide excess profits 60% / 40% respectively. The investors likely receive a lower pref, in comparison to a pari-passu pref, because it is a true pref.

Common Equity with a Pari-Passu Pref

Capital Contribution:	
Sponsor	10%
Investors	90%
Distribution Priority:	
First	To investors and sponsor until they reach an 8% annualized return
Second	Return of capital
Third	75% to investors, 25% to sponsor

In this example of a common equity investment with a pari-passu pref, the investors and sponsor each receive an 8% annualized return on their investments and return of capital, pro rata. Above the 8% pari-passu pref, investors and sponsor divide excess profits 75% / 25% respectively. In this case, investors do not receive any profits before the sponsor does. The pari-passu pref allows the sponsor to receive cash flow alongside the investors during the investment period. The investors' repayment risk is higher, but they also share in more of the profits. In this scenario, the investors are treated as equal to the sponsor until the pref is paid and capital is returned. Beyond that point, the sponsor earns a disproportionate share of additional profits via its promote.

Simple v. Cumulative Pref

The final item of note is that the pref is not always calculated in the same way. Sometimes, the sponsor calculates the pref on a simple interest basis. The alternative is a compounding basis. Supposed that an investor is entitled to a 10% annual pref, but that in the first year, there is only enough profit to pay a 5% return. In the second year, cash flow ramps substantially and pays a 15% return. In the simple interest basis, the additional 5% would still be owed next year but not added to the initial balance. In the compounding basis, the outstanding 5% would be added to the investor's capital account for purposes of calculating the next years preferred return. This example is shown below.

Non-compounding

	Year 1	Year 2
Initial Balance	$100,000	$105,000
Amount owed	$10,000	$10,000
Amount paid	$5,000	$15,000
Ending Balance	$105,000	$100,000

Compounding

	Year 1	Year 2
Initial Balance	$100,000	$105,000
Amount owed	$10,000	$10,500
Amount paid	$5,000	$15,000
Ending Balance	$105,000	$100,000

Notice in the compounding example, even the ramped up 15% return did not satisfy the accumulated return owed. It fell short by $500, which would then be compounded into the pref accrued for Year 3. Over time, the compounded pref can generate substantially greater returns in the case of operating shortfalls in earlier years.

What is a Cap Rate?

The capitalization, or "cap" rate is a term that is used frequently when discussing real estate asset sales and purchases. The cap rate is a ratio of two variables – net operating income and the current value or sale price of a property – which helps to determine the potential return on an investment. Put another way, the cap rate is the rate at which the net operating income recapitalizes the asset value on an annual basis. The cap rate is a useful tool that is often used to assess real estate investment opportunities and draw conclusions across asset classes.

The capitalization, or "cap" rate is a term that is used frequently when discussing real estate asset sales and purchases. The cap rate is a ratio of two variables – net operating income and the current value or sale price of a property – which helps to determine the potential return on an investment. Another way to contemplate the cap rate is that it is the rate at which the net operating income recapitalizes the asset value on an annual basis.

Capitalization Rate = Net Operating Income (NOI) / Current Market Value (or Sale Price)

For example, if an investment group buys an apartment property in Los Angeles with an annual NOI of $1,000,000 for $20 million the cap rate is 5%:

$1,000,000 / $20,000,000 = 5%

Also, as noted above, the asset is producing 5% of its value in income every year. At this rate, the asset will pay for itself in 20 years.

How are cap rates used?

Cap rates are used in various ways when analyzing real estate investments. Investment groups use cap rates internally to compare and contrast investment opportunities. For example, that same investment group can spend that $20 million to buy the Los Angeles apartment building at a 5% cap rate. Or, it may consider spending $14 million to buy a shopping center in Kansas City at a 7% cap rate and the remaining $6 million to buy an industrial building in Minneapolis at a 6.5% cap. There are a number of other factors that go into those real estate decisions, but on a purely numbers basis, the investment group can weigh the pros and cons of buying one asset in a top market that will deliver a 5% return, or buy two different assets in smaller cities with a higher blended return of 6.85%.

Cap rates also are used as a benchmark to gauge industry trends across asset classes related to pricing. In that regard, cap rates can show supply and demand and what buyers are willing to pay for properties and over time, they can be useful to discern patterns or breakouts.

As an illustrative example, the following graph produced by Market Realist, does an excellent job of comparing historical cap rates across five major asset classes from 2010 - 2015:

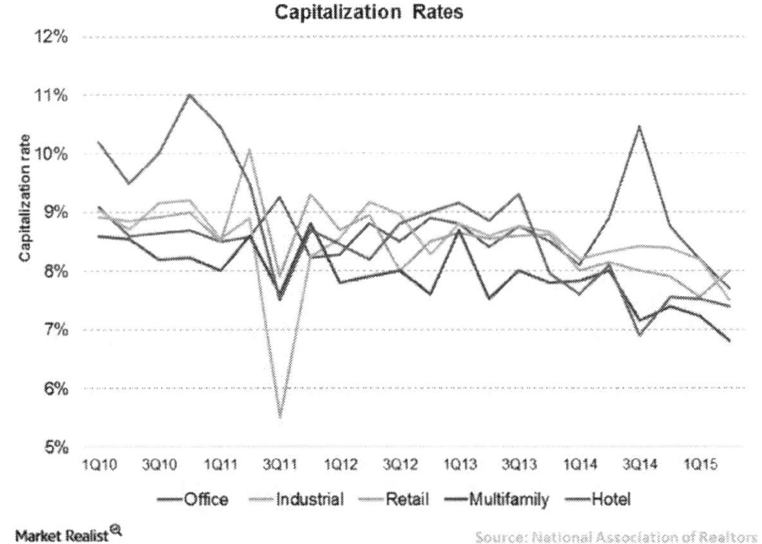

As the graph clearly depicts, cap rates across all asset classes compressed, on average, about 160 basis points from Q1 2010 to Q1 2015. The takeaway from this first point is to know that if you purchased any real estate asset in Q1 2015, you accepted a lower yield (i.e. NOI as a lower percentage of purchase price) compared to what you would have received in Q1 2010. The vastly improved economic conditions in 2015 vs. the near abyss of 2010 may have well justified the lower yield (we cover this topic in our chapter, "What are Real Estate Risk-Adjusted Returns?") but it is a fact nonetheless.

In addition, amongst the five major asset classes, another takeaway is that, as of Q1 2015, multifamily assets were trading at cap rates that were 60 basis to 120 basis lower than other asset classes. Again, your opinion might have been that the desirability of multifamily assets more than justified this spread but the fact remains that, if you invested in a multifamily project in Q1 2015, you accepted a lower yield than you could have obtained by investing in a similar quality retail or office project.

What else do I need to know?

> "The cap rate is one of two metrics (the other being NOI) commonly used to value commercial real estate. In this section, I define the cap rate and describe how they are used in real estate private equity."
>
> 
> Ian Formigle

While cap rates are a good metric to compare and contrast different investment opportunities, as well as a good measure of market trends it is important to note that not everyone calculates NOI in the same way. Some investors use 12-month trailing income while others will make assumptions based on predictions of higher income in the next 12 months. This is referred to as trailing vs. forward-looking cap rates. Altering these assumptions can produce radically different cap rate results. In some respects, this discrepancy partially explains why investors are willing to pay very low cap rates of below 4%. When accepting a sub 4% cap rate, the investor is less focused on the trailing cap rate and, instead, is targeting a substantially higher forward-looking cap rate. That investor has likely underwritten the acquisition with an expectation that they can boost NOI by raising rents or lease current vacancies. This future improved cap rate is referred to as the "stabilized cap rate".

Conversely, the purchase price may not be a direct reflection of the NOI that supports it. Suppose a suburban office building requires significant capital improvements. That office building might sell for a lower price since the next buyer will need to invest a large sum into those capital improvements upon acquisition simply to retain the current tenants at current rents (rather than improve the property to increase rents). In that scenario, a higher cap rate is justified compared to a similarly situated office that does not have major deferred maintenance issues even if the NOI is the same for each.

In short, the cap rate is a useful tool that is often used alongside other criteria to assess real estate investment opportunities and draw conclusions across asset classes. Keep in mind that understanding how NOI relates to cap rates is critical in utilizing cap rates as a resource as well as understanding that cap rates are an estimated return that can change over time.

The Yin and Yang of Equity Multiples and IRR

Equity multiples and internal rate of return (IRR) are two important metrics to measure investment returns that are used in tandem. Each is an important analysis tool on its own. But combined, they provide even more insight on the potential benefits of a real estate investment.

Equity multiples and internal rate of return (IRR) are two important metrics to measure investment returns that are used in tandem. Each is an important analysis tool on its own. But combined, they provide even more insight on the potential benefits of a real estate investment.

One of the keys to understanding IRR is realizing that timing plays an important role. The time or duration of the investment hold period and the timing that cash distributions are paid to investors both have a big influence on this equation. More details on IRR can be found in our chapter "Understanding Internal Rate of Return (IRR) in Real Estate Investing".

What is an Equity Multiple?

In real estate, equity multiples are used primarily as a measure of the total return paid to an investor. The equity multiple is found by dividing the cumulative distributions from a project by the paid-in capital. The equity multiple differs from the IRR in that it does not take into account the length of the investment period or the time value of money.

> "An IRR and equity multiple, each only tell part of the story of targeted returns. In this section, I explain why they must be used in tandem to truly understand the story."
>
> 
> Ian Formigle

Equity multiple = cumulative distributed returns / paid-in capital

Equity multiples and IRR are closely intertwined in real estate private equity. Another notable difference is that the equity multiple is static, while the IRR is variable. For example, if an investor puts in $100,000 and gets $200,000 back in total return, that is a 2x equity multiple - period. It has no bearing on how long it took to earn that return. It is a valuable exercise to overlay an equity multiple with IRR to get a sense of the total return that also accounts for the timing of the payout on that return. The faster an investor gets that return, the higher the IRR. If an investor gets 100% of that return – all $200K – in one year, that is a 100% IRR. However, if the investor receives that return in 5 years, the 2x multiple doesn't change, but the IRR drops, perhaps to 20%, depending on the timing of distributions.

As this example shows, all IRRs are not created equally. That is why it is important to look at IRRs in conjunction with equity multiples as a measure of total returns. Other key points to understand as to why it is important to look at both metrics include:

The IRR is something that can be manipulated. That is an important consideration when looking at a sponsor promote structure that is IRR driven. A sponsor may be able to quickly hit an IRR target that will trigger payment of a sponsor promote, even if that means falling short of a projected equity multiple.

In some deals, the equity multiples can provide an added layer of checks and balances by requiring the sponsor to achieve both an IRR and a certain level of equity multiple before the sponsor becomes eligible to receive a promote. You sometimes see this type of hurdle layered into an institutional JV co-investment structure.

Investors may value equity multiples and IRR differently depending on their investment objectives. Investors that are more yield-driven may favor offerings with a higher IRR, whereas investors who focus on building long-term wealth may place greater emphasis on deals with a higher equity multiple.

CrowdStreet makes a point to include both equity multiples and IRR targets as part of its offering information to provide transparency to accredited investors. We also show you both metrics, because we understand that investors have different objectives. Having both metrics helps investors to better compare and contrast investment offerings and make a selection that best fits individual investment objectives.

What is a Real Estate Sponsor Promote?

A key term to a real estate private equity deal is the sponsor "promote". This term is really just industry jargon for the sponsor's disproportionate share of profits in a real estate deal above a predetermined return threshold. In this chapter, we will define the sponsor promote, explore how promotes work, explain how they are justified as well as how they benefit both sponsors and investors and, finally, what they mean to investors under a direct-to-investor model.

A key term to a real estate private equity deal is the sponsor "promote". This term is really just industry jargon for the sponsor's disproportionate share of profits in a real estate deal above a predetermined return threshold. In almost any other form of alternative investment, a sponsor promote is referred to as "carried interest". In this chapter, we will define the sponsor promote, explore how promotes work, explain how they are justified as well as how they benefit both sponsors and investors and, finally, what they mean to investors under a direct-to-investor model, like the offerings on our marketplace.

Real estate sponsors usually invest their own capital into a deal alongside their equity co-investors. While it is possible for sponsors to subordinate their own capital to that of their investors, it is far more typical that they earn the exact same returns (this is known as being "pari passu") as the other equity investors until they reach a certain return threshold ("known as the "preferred return"). Above the preferred return, sponsors will begin to divide excess profits disproportionately in their favor. The amount of money paid to the sponsor above the amount earned on his/her contributed capital to the deal is the promote.

Example: A sponsor contributes 10% of his own capital as part of the total equity required to acquire a property and raises the remaining 90% of total equity from other investors. The sponsor contributes his 10% of equity in the same entity as the other 90% of co-investors. Therefore, "Members" is 100% of equity. Also, the sponsor is the General Partner, and the investors are Limited Partners.

Below is a detailed look at the priority of distributions and profit sharing, known as the "waterfall" that includes the sponsor promote and an explanation of each tier:

Distribution Waterfall

First, 100% pro rata to the Members until each member has received an amount equal to a 10% IRR preferred return and its unrecovered capital contribution

Explanation: Since the sponsor has contributed 10% of total equity alongside his co-investors, this first tier of the waterfall splits revenues on a 90% (investors) / 10% (sponsor co-invest) basis until everyone has received a full return of capital plus a 10% annualized compounded rate of return. This first tier is the preferred return.

Second, 75% to the Members until each member has received an amount equal to a 20% IRR, and 25% to the General Partner as Promoted Interest.

"Promotes are how commercial real estate operators earn most of their compensation in commercial real estate deals. In this section, I explain how promotes are calculated and why they are warranted."

Ian Formigle

Explanation: This is the first tier of the promote. Above a 10% IRR, the sponsor now earns 25% of all excess profits over and above the sponsor's pro-rata share of his own profits from his 10% equity contribution. This disproportionate profit split continues until the Members receive a 20% IRR. Another way to look at this second tier is on a pure investors vs. sponsor split basis. Since investors contributed 90% of total equity, then at the second tier, they receive 75% of 90% or 67.5% of excess profits above a 10% IRR up to a 20% IRR. The sponsor receives the balance or 32.5% of excess profits above a 10% IRR up to a 20% IRR, which is inclusive of his 10% equity contribution.

Thereafter, any remaining net cash shall be distributed 60% to the Members and 40% to the General Partner as Promoted Interest.

Explanation: This is the second and final tier of the promote. Above a 20% IRR to all equity, the sponsor now earns 40% of all excess profits. When looking at it from the pure investor vs. sponsor split perspective, this would mean that investors receive 60% of 90% or 54% of profits above a 20% IRR and the sponsor receives 46% of excess profits above a 20% IRR, which is inclusive of his 10% equity contribution.

Why does the sponsor deserve to earn a promote?

An investor might look at the waterfall structure detailed above and think, "If the property performs exceptionally well, the sponsor stands to make a lot more money in this transaction than investors." However, it is important to remember that investors are relying upon the sponsor, among other things, to do the following:

Source and identify assets

Underwrite and discover hidden value

Pursue, negotiate and win deals

Develop asset business plans

Negotiate purchase and sale agreements

Conduct thorough due diligence

Secure financing

Close deals

Manage assets

Lease to new tenants

Renew leases with existing tenants

Perform and manage capital expenditure projects

Execute asset business plans

Dispose of assets; and

Deliver investment returns

Considering that the sponsor does all of the heavy lifting in a deal while investors are paid a preferred return or are "unpromoted" up until a hurdle return, it is logical for the sponsor to expect to earn a greater share of profits than their pro-rata equity participation would otherwise suggest.

Win-win scenario

The sponsor promote incentivizes sponsors to exceed expectations and beat the original pro forma or business plan. If a sponsor beats expectations, their bonus is earned in the form of the promote. Equity investors also share in those additional profits but to a lesser degree. Because investors rely on the sponsor to execute upon the items listed above, they want to incentivize the sponsor to keep his/her eye on the prize, and the carrot of disproportionate profits participation is a strong incentive.

It also is important to note that a promote structure can vary depending on the sponsor and the type of property. Generally speaking, the more the sponsor has to work to generate the targeted returns and/or have the greater the complexity of the deal, the more favorable the splits of the promote will be for that deal.

Finally, keep in mind that a promote is separate and distinct from fees that a sponsor may earn in a deal, which can include acquisition fees, asset management fees and, potentially, disposition fees.

The direct to investor difference

One of the advantages of a direct-to-investor platform is that there is only one promote, which is paid to the sponsor. Platforms that use a special purpose vehicle (SPV) model to list offerings may also include a second promote. In this double-promoted structure, project profits are split twice- once between the platform and sponsor, and once between the platform and investor- before the investor receives anything. The CrowdStreet Marketplace, however uses a direct to investor platform that does not charge a second promote. Targeted returns displayed on CrowdStreet Marketplace offerings are "net-to-investor," meaning that the numbers displayed are reflective of the sponsor promote.

Prior to making an investment decision, it is important to understand the sponsor promote including tiers and splits and whether or not that is the only promote in the deal. CrowdStreet's policy is that a sponsor must be fully transparent regarding offering information. Specifics on the sponsor promote may always be found on the detail page under the Summary of Terms tab.

Shining a Spotlight on Real Estate Sponsor Fees

Sponsors do a fair amount of work to put a deal together, manage it throughout its life cycle, and execute on a business plan to produce a favorable outcome for stakeholders. So, it's no surprise that they want to get paid for those efforts. For real estate projects, sponsors have two primary compensation methods: 1) a profits interest or "promote" and 2) fees. Much like other investment metrics, the way the fees are structured can help to paint a picture of the overall project and provide another window on risk vs. return. In this chapter, we highlight the differences between fees and profit interests and provide some of the most common justifications for fees typical seen in commercial real estate investments.

Sponsors do a fair amount of work to put a deal together, manage a deal throughout its life cycle, and execute on a business plan to produce a favorable outcome for stakeholders. So, it is no surprise that they should want to get paid for those efforts. For real estate projects, sponsors have two primary compensation methods: 1) a profits interest or "promote" and 2) fees. Much like other investment metrics, the way the fees are structured can help to paint a picture of the overall project.

Fee vs. Profit Interest

Sponsor compensation can take two forms: fees and promote. While a promote is realized after a project meets certain goals (see our chapter, "What is a Real Estate Sponsor Promote?"), fees can be collected at different stages of a project regardless of whether or not it is meeting expectations. Also, fees are typically taken out before profits are calculated for purposes of an equity waterfall (see our chapter, "Understanding the Real Estate Capital Stack"). Finally, fees are usually tied to specific tasks that the sponsor performs, such as negotiating and closing a property purchase, rather than overall project success.

Different types of fees

Because they are typically assessed for discrete tasks, the permutations of fees can be myriad, especially if a project is particularly complex. In addition, some fees may be set as a flat amount or a percentage of cost. Some of the fees, such as a property management fee, could be shopped out to a third party. If a sponsor has in-house capabilities (this is known as being "vertically integrated"), the sponsor can create efficiencies that result in lower costs. They then arbitrage the difference through their internal fees.

> "After promotes, sponsor fees are the other way the other way operators are compensated in deals. In this section, I walk you through the types of fees typically found in deals and explain how they differ from promotes."
>
> Ian Formigle

Below, we discuss some but, by no means all, of the typical sponsor fees.

Acquisition / Disposition: These fees relate specifically to the purchase and sale of property or land. It is usually a one-time transaction fee that is collected after the purchase or sale and may come in addition to or in lieu of a third-party broker commission, depending upon whether the sponsor has in-house broker capabilities. Although a sponsor may choose to split out a separate finding fee, the acquisition fee often helps to cover the costs associated with finding and evaluating potential assets. Sponsors often underwrite and pursue dozens of potential candidates for each actual acquisition, so the spirit of this fee is to help the sponsor to defray sunk costs on all the properties it did not acquire (known as "dead deal" costs). The logic behind an acquisition fee is that investors should want to incentivize a sponsor to acquire the best deals and not the first deal that lands in its lap. Disposition fees, when assessed, are often viewed as the other half of sharing deal costs. Market acquisition and disposition fees vary and can be up to 2% of the purchase or sale price.

Property Management: Sponsors may do their own in-house property management, meaning they are in charge of day-to-day operations, maintenance, leasing, and upkeep of a building or property. Having in-house property management is another way of showing vertical integration. Of course, many sponsors prefer to contract these responsibilities to 3rd-party firms. Market rates for property management fees range from 3% - 4% of gross revenues, typically paid monthly in arrears for the duration of the investment period.

Asset Management: The asset management fee is most closely associated with general investment management costs. Much as the property manager executes the day-to-day operations at the property level, the asset manager oversees operations and makes decisions regarding the asset itself, such as choosing a property manager, determining and adjusting the asset strategy, making key decisions on leasing and capital expenditures, reviewing and approving property-level expenditures above a certain threshold (typically $1,000), reviewing monthly accounting reports, and making recommendations to an investment committee on when to sell or refinance. Asset management fees are usually assessed monthly or quarterly during the investment period and are either a fixed amount or a percentage of the equity raised or a fixed percentage of gross revenues. Market rates average about 1 - 2% of gross revenues or equity annually.

Construction Management: Sponsors may charge construction fees if there is significant renovation or ground-up construction as part of an asset business plan. In projects involving construction, the sponsor does a tremendous amount of project management, which can include working directly with a general contractor or subcontractors to determine the scope of work, gather and negotiate bids, hire and fire contractors, make key decisions along the way (e.g. interior finishes), review monthly cost reports, approve installment payments, make decisions on any change orders (usually with consent of Investment Committees), inspect progress, and approve completion. Construction management fees typically average 5% of hard construction costs or less (see our chapter, "Sources & Uses: Following the Real Estate Money Trail").

Development: Development fees pertain to the entirety of the building process and may involve a variety of pre-construction steps, such as environmental testing, securing zoning, obtaining building approvals and permits and hiring architects, engineers and contractors to complete the work. Sponsors typically charge development fees as a percentage of either hard costs or total development costs, including soft costs. They may also charge a flat rate if the project is relatively "cookie-cutter". A project sponsor who lacks the expertise to manage pre-development or construction tasks may hire a third-party "fee developer" to manage the development process. Development fees vary and can range from 3% to 5% of total cost often with smaller percentages charged on larger projects.

The relative weight that a sponsor gives to fees rather than profits interest can give an investor insight into how the sponsor views itself. For instance, a vertically-integrated firm may charge more fees and rely less on profit interest, particularly if the sponsor is well-established with a proven track record. However, a smaller, more focused outfit might charge fewer fees during the project lifecycle but take a greater promote. Such a structure aligns well with investors when sponsors are less proven as it makes total compensation to the sponsor more dependent upon performance.

It is important to look at sponsor fees in the broader context of the whole deal, including the work a sponsor is doing and the complexity of a deal, along with the targeted returns. It is also important for investors to keep in mind that, while low fees are always a nicety in a deal, it is difficult to escape the idiom of "you get what you pay for". Sponsors who charge higher than average fees have usually earned the right to do so, since, investors care most about net returns and care less about sponsor fees if returns are strong and consistent. When there are little to no fees involved, whether or not you think it is the case, you are likely trading a low fee structure for something else in a deal (e.g. lack of sponsor experience or a handsome promote structure where the sponsor likes the odds of the upside scenario). Ultimately, investors must rely on their judgement to determine whether a given fee is fair.

Sponsor fees can easily get lost or buried in the middle of offering documents. As part of its commitment to transparency, CrowdStreet required sponsors to list all fees on a dedicated tab in its detail pages. That way, investors can compare them across offerings.

Understanding the Real Estate Capital Stack

One of the most valuable tools available to investors for evaluating and comprehending risk in direct real estate investments is the "capital stack". For the purposes of commercial real estate, the capital stack is the different layers of financing sources that go into funding the purchase and improvement of a real estate project. Ideally, a real estate investment hits its business plan or pro forma target and everybody gets paid according to plan. But, like any investment, real estate has downside risk. The capital stack provides investors with valuable information about where they fall in the pecking order of cash flows, what that order means for risk of repayment and, ultimately, whether the targeted return on investment is worth the assumed risk.

One of the most valuable tools available to investors for evaluating and comprehending risk in direct real estate investments is the "capital stack". For the purposes of commercial real estate, the capital stack is the different layers of financing sources that go into funding the purchase and improvement of a real estate project. Ideally, a real estate investment hits its business plan or pro forma target and everybody gets paid according to plan. But, like any investment, real estate has downside risk. The capital stack provides investors with valuable information about where they fall in the pecking order of cash flows, what that order means for risk of repayment and, ultimately, whether the targeted return on investment is worth the assumed risk.

While there is theoretically no limit to the number of layers a capital stacks may contain , we will keep our analysis to the four most commonly used types of capital in ascending order of priority:

When analyzing the capital stack depicted above, here is the road map for understanding it:

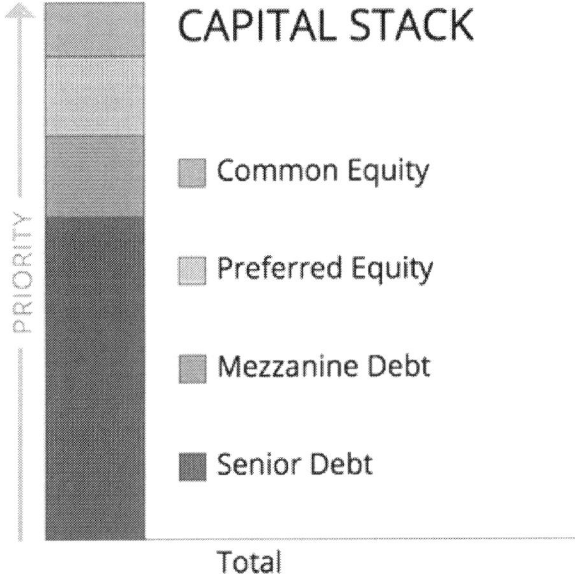

Each capital source has seniority over all capital sources located above it in the capital stack.

Each capital source is subordinate to all capital sources located below it in the capital stack.

Typically, only the senior and junior debt* positions are able to secure recorded liens against the underlying asset.

Upon sale or refinance, the bottom position gets paid first until fully repaid and so on.

To the extent that there are insufficient funds to fully repay all capital then losses are incurred from the top down.

This means that risk increases as you move higher in the capital stack. This also means that returns should increase as you move higher in the capital stack.

Sponsor co-investments are most typically contributed as equity at the highest position in the capital stack.

A good way to think about how capital stacks relate to repayment is to imagine a rectangular prism that is full of water. At purchase, pour the water into a separate container. If things start to go awry, begin removing water from the separate container. If they begin to go better, replace some of the water in the separate container. If things go great, keep adding water to the separate container. Upon sale, pour the water from the separate container back into the rectangular prism. If you fill the entire prism and it begins to spill over, the amount of spillover is your profit! If it exactly refills the rectangular prism, then everyone is repaid but you broke even. If it fails to refill the entire prism then the unfilled portion is your loss and the owners of the unfilled area are the investors in the deal that have incurred the loss.

> "The "Cap Stack" as it is commonly referred to within the industry, is the preeminent tool for discerning the financial pecking order within a deal. In this section, I provide the primary elements of the Cap Stack as well as a roadmap for interpreting it."
>
> Ian Formigle

While the capital stack depicted above has four layers, capital stacks more commonly have fewer layers with the most common being two layers.

For example, think of the financing that goes into buying a home. Typically, a home buyer takes out a mortgage and makes a cash down payment for the balance of the purchase. The mortgage might provide 75% of the total purchase price (the debt portion of the capital stack) while the homeowner contributes the remaining 25% (the equity portion of the capital stack).

Assuming a $400,000 purchase price, that capital stack looks like this:

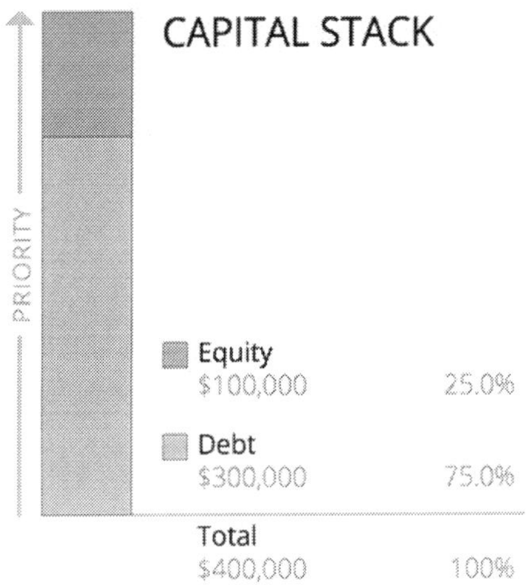

Fast forward a number of years, and the homeowner now wants to build a new addition. So, she decides to take out a second mortgage, particularly because the real estate market has been kind to her as the home she purchased for $400,000 just appraised for $500,000. The original lender maintains a first position at the bottom of the stack. The new mortgage slots into the second position and the homeowner is now in third position atop the capital stack with her increased equity (we refer to this increase as "imputed equity"). Assuming that the first mortgage has experienced $25,000 of amortization since purchase, the new capital stack for that same home now looks like this:

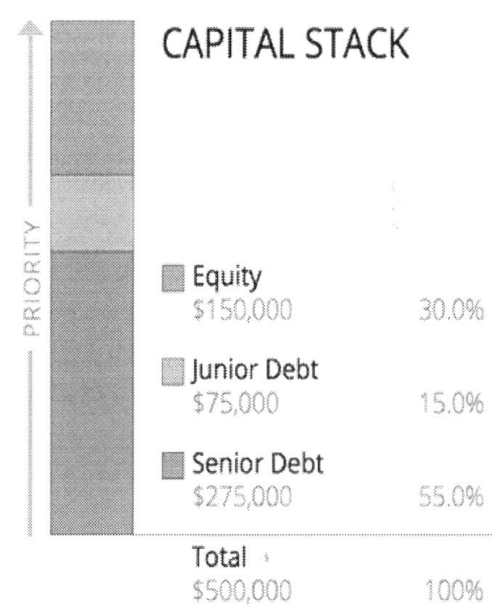

It is important for investors to understand that in a well-constructed capital stack, there is no right or wrong position but, rather, positions that incur more risk or less risk and, in exchange, pay out larger or smaller rewards. By understanding the capital stack, you become empowered to make an informed as to where you feel comfortable in the capital stack as well as whether the risk relative to each position is commensurate with the potential reward. For this reason, every offering posted on the CrowdStreet Marketplace will include a cleanly articulated capital stack.

As investors grow and diversify their real estate portfolios, it is common to participate in different layers of the capital stack in both debt and equity investment opportunities as a means to spread out risk and generate higher blended returns. The CrowdStreet Marketplace offers accredited investors the opportunity to invest at different points in the capital stack such as first position debt, mezzanine financing and equity investments.

Real Estate Investment Strategy: Four Categories of Risk & Reward

Within private equity real estate, assets are typically grouped into four primary categories based on investment strategy and perceived risk. Those four categories are core, core-plus, value-added and opportunistic. The key differentiator between these categories is the risk and return profile. Moving between these strategies is a bit like stepping up the ladder in terms of taking on more risk, and in theory, being compensated for that risk with a higher return. In this chapter, we describe each category and outline the typical level of leverage used for each in order to clearly illustrate the concepts involved.

Within private equity real estate, assets are typically grouped into four primary strategy categories based on investment strategy and perceived risk. Those four categories are core, core-plus, value-added and opportunistic. The key differentiator between these categories is the risk and return profile. Moving between those strategies is a bit like stepping up the ladder in terms of taking on more risk, and in theory, being compensated for that risk with a higher return. We describe each category and outline the typical level of leverage (see our chapter, "Leverage: The Double-edged Sword of Real Estate Finance") used for each category below but also acknowledge that the use of leverage is determined by lenders and borrowers and, therefore, can vary from the ranges discussed below.

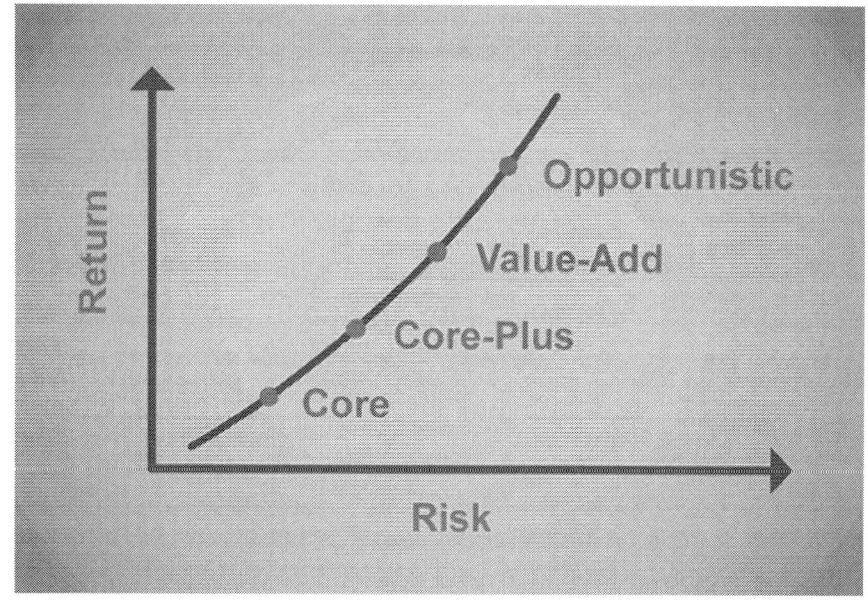

Core: Core assets, considered the safest, sit at the bottom of the risk-return ladder. Core properties are relatively stable assets in major metros, such as high-rise office towers or apartment buildings downtown locations in New York City, Chicago, San Francisco, Washington D.C. or L.A. They are usually best-in-class properties in the best locations, with high, stable occupancy and credit tenants. Core assets can be quite large and expensive and, therefore, are usually owned by well-capitalized entities, such as REITs and other institutional investors. Because they are stabilized and already achieve market rents, there is not much value an investor can add, which obviously limits their upside. However, in an economic downturn, they are usually the last to lose tenants. As a result, due to a lack of value-added opportunities that also offer a low risk profile, core investments usually translate to single-digit annual returns.

Leverage with Core: Can range from 0% to 50% of asset value and rarely higher. The reason for low leverage with core is that it is simply not conducive to the use of much leverage given its low unleveraged returns. Leveraging core assets adds little to leveraged returns so it typically adds more risk than return.

Core-Plus: Core-plus strategy assets occupy the next rung in the risk ladder. Core-plus assets may share many of the same characteristics with core assets with one or more exceptions that create added risk. Some examples of those exceptions might include the age or condition of the asset, a dip in tenant credit or less than stellar location. For example, that Chicago office tower might be two or three blocks off Main & Main, or it might be a historic building rather than new construction. Annualized leveraged returns on these assets are generally range from 10% - 14%.

> "Once you understand the basics of each asset class, it's time to begin understanding different risk profiles in each asset class. In this section, I walk you through each of the four risk profiles and provide guidance on the typical amount of leverage used in each profile."
>
> 
> Ian Formigle

Leverage with Core-Plus: 50% - 65% of asset value. Unleveraged returns on Core-plus assets are high enough to justify the use of leverage to increase leveraged returns. However, leverage is typically limited in order to limit risk and preserve the overall risk-reward balance of a Core-plus profile.

Value-added: Value-added assets take a bigger step out in the risk-reward line. Value-added assets generally have a problem that needs fixing, such as leasing to improve significant vacancy, renovation or re-tenanting to improve the quality of the rent roll. The purchaser is usually coming in with a specific business plan to improve an under-utilized asset. One example is a shopping center that has lost an anchor tenant, such as a grocery store or other big box tenant. The purchaser will have an opportunity to buy that property at a discount given the absence of an anchor. If the new owner has an effective business plan to reposition the anchor space (possibly by demising it into two to three spaces) and bring new tenants to the property that would improve the overall shopping experience, the new owner can make a substantial profit. Just think of what reformatting a former Albertsons into a combination of a Trader Joe's and a Bed, Bath and Beyond would do for the overall shopping experience and how it would drive traffic to the entire center. A well-executed strategy can turn a value-add asset into a core-plus property. With more risk and effort required to successfully execute the business plan, these investments often provide leveraged returns in the high teens at 15% - 19%.

Leverage with Value-added: 65% - 85% of asset value. Unleveraged returns on Value-added assets are now high enough to entice additional use of leverage to further enhance leveraged returns. In addition, re-tenanting and repositioning strategies, as described above, can often be mostly capitalized through additional leverage that is funded by the senior lender post closing as the business plan is proven out. In industry jargon, we refer to this as "future funding" or "good news money".

Opportunistic: Opportunistic assets are the final rung at the top of the risk ladder. These deals are generally extreme turnaround situations. There are major problems to overcome, such as major vacancy, structural issues or financial distress. Sometimes referred to as Distressed Assets, Opportunistic strategies may involve acquiring foreclosed assets from banks or servicers or acquiring the senior loan at a discount from banks or servicers with an eye toward eventual foreclosure. Opportunistic investments were plentiful in the wake of the recession as bold investors stepped in to buy properties in distress at a steep discounts from previous trades. In some cases, opportunistic deals require special expertise to execute the turn around or patience to wait out a downturn in the market to effect a value-added strategy once tenant demand begins to resurface. Because opportunistic investments carry the highest risk and require the greatest expertise, they can provide annualized leveraged returns of over 20%.

Leverage with Opportunistic: 0% - 70% of asset value. Because of the distressed nature of Opportunistic strategy assets, they are often ineligible for much (and sometimes any) leverage upon acquisition. If you acquired a note, you essentially bought the leveraged part of the deal with a strategy to convert it to a low basis unleveraged asset. The broad range is due to the fact that Opportunistic strategies are highly case dependent. Opportunistic assets may also start with little to no leverage but find their way to leverage or increased leverage as the business plan develops. Think of a situation in which you acquire a 100,000 SF vacant retail building (this is often referred to as a "dark box") for $3 million or $30/SF all cash that could be worth $18 million or $180/SF with a stable NNN tenant on a long term lease. However, that tenant will require $7 million of tenant improvements and capital improvements in order to entice them to occupy the property. With a signed lease in hand, you could approach a lender, pledge the unleveraged building as collateral and obtain a loan for the entire $7 million needed to perform the work to install the tenant. Once the tenant takes occupancy, you have now a Core-plus asset.

What are the takeaways?

It is important for investors to understand the risk and return relationship when discussing the four different types of real estate investment strategies. The level of the return should be commensurate with the amount of risk. Specific to value-add and opportunistic deals, investors also need to keep in mind that the expertise of the sponsor and their ability to create and execute a business plan can be critical to the success of a project.

A well-balanced commercial real estate portfolio may include some or even all of these different investment categories depending on the risk tolerance of the individual investor.

Top 10 Sources of Risk in Real Estate Investment Deals

Risk is the elephant in the room when it comes to private real estate offerings. It's open discussion is often skirted at the outset of a proposed investment opportunity and, in some instances, vastly underestimated. While avoiding investment risk is ideal, unless investors want to simply hold treasuries (which is generally referred to as the "risk free rate of return"), the reality is that risk is a natural part of any investment and commercial real estate is no exception. In this chapter we walk you through the ten most common source of risk present in commercial real estate investment opportunities. After reading, you should better understand the relative levels of risk present in the opportunities you evaluate and be able to insure you are being adequately compensated through appropriate risk-adjusted returns.

Risk is the elephant in the room when it comes to private real estate offerings. Its open discussion is often skirted at the outset of a proposed investment opportunity and, in some instances, vastly underestimated. While avoiding investment risk is ideal, unless investors want to simply hold treasuries (which is generally referred to as the "risk free rate of return"), the reality is that risk is a natural part of any investment and commercial real estate is no exception.

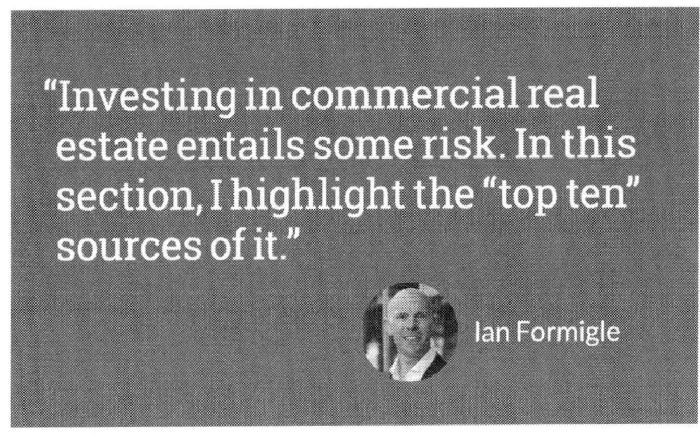

So, rather than pretend that every investment will experience the "good deal" exemption, it is wiser to confront the issue head-on by recognizing where risks exist, estimating how big those risks are and determining whether or not you, as an investor, are getting sufficiently compensated for assuming that level of risk. The first step is understanding the different types of risks that can pop-up to negatively affect a real estate investment. At a macro level, there are a number of broad geopolitical and economic events that can derail a potential investment. Since investors have no control over such events and they are nearly impossible to predict, this chapter will, instead, focus on the top ten micro or "deal" level risks that are more easily compared and contrasted across competing investments choices.

When evaluating a real estate investment, it is important to consider the following ten elements of risk:

Sponsor risk: The experience and ability of the developer, operator or lender can have a substantive impact on whether that sponsor can execute on a business plan and deliver targeted results to stakeholders. Within sponsor risk, there are two primary subsets:

> **Asset management risk:** The asset manager is charged with executing the business plan at a strategic level. The asset manager's expertise and attentiveness to the asset is paramount in translating a business plan into a successful outcome.
>
> **Property management risk:** Assets that require individual customer service as an important part of executing a business plan (e.g. multifamily, senior housing, hospitality and storage) are highly dependent upon property management. In these scenarios, outstanding property management is critical as the day-to-day onsite operations of the asset will have a direct effect on its performance.

Debt risks: Placing debt on a project is a common practice but placing too much debt on it or having it mature at an inopportune time can imperil it, particularly in the event of a market downturn (see market risk below). Debt risks can lead to foreclosure. Foreclosure isn't as much of a risk itself but the unfortunate outcome of the incurred risks of over leverage, debt maturity or a combination of both.

Over leverage: If a property loses too many tenants its net operating income can drop to the point that its debt coverage service ratio can fall below 1.0, which now places the asset into risk of defaulting on its mortgage. Prudent leverage on an asset can range anywhere from 0% to 80% depending on the asset strategy (see: Real Estate Investment Strategy: Four Categories of Risk & Reward). If an asset is leveraged in excess of 80% of value then it should have a compelling justification for the use of that much leverage. Otherwise, it may be overleveraged.

Debt maturity risk: If a property's debt matures in a down market (see market risk below) or at a point when its net operating income is compromised, as noted above, then the project may be unable to obtain a new loan in the same amount of the outstanding debt. If investors are unable to infuse the additional capital necessary to refinance the project then the asset is now in risk of mortgage default. Debt maturity was one of the major culprits of why projects were lost during the financial crisis.

Cap rate risk: Of all the financial assumptions in a pro forma, cap rate risk is the most extreme since it has a dramatic effect on an asset's exit value, and that is why it is included in this list. As I illustrated in my articleour chapter, "What is a Cap Rate?", prevailing cap rates for different asset classes move in ranges and are subject to supply and demand for that particular asset class. A small movement in a cap rate percentage can have a substantial effect on the residual value of an asset and, in turn, the profitability (or loss) on a particular transaction. When analyzing an investment opportunity, pay attention to the entry and exit cap rates and ask yourself 1) is the entry cap rate attractive for this asset when compared to its competitive set and 2) the assumed exit cap rate is defensible over the prescribed holding period?

Tenant risk: There are two primary subsets of tenant risk: a) rent roll quality and b) rollover risk:

> Rent roll quality - this usually refers to credit worthiness, stability and number of tenants. Do the tenants of a particular property have staying power, or could the tenant(s) go out of business, file bankruptcy or default on its lease? Generally, large national tenants such as Google or Amazon are viewed as highly desirable and less risky compared to mom-and-pop start-ups. Another element of tenant risk is single tenant vs. multi-tenant scenarios. Single tenants can be great during a lease term since your property, by definition is 100% leased but if they default or vacate at expiration, your property is now 100% vacant. In contrast, multi-tenant buildings are rarely 100% leased or 100% vacant. By creating a diverse tenant mix where no single tenant occupies more than 20% of the total leasable area of a building and staggering lease expirations, you can mitigate occupancy risk and help to ensure your building remains mostly occupied at all times regardless of what happens with any single tenant.
>
> Rollover risk - this refers to the remaining term left on leases at a property and it affects both single tenant and multi-tenant properties. Logically speaking, more term is better but that aspect of leases is often priced into assets, so it's not as easy as simply looking for longest

term leases you can find. In addition, acquiring a property with a tenant on a long-term lease that then defaults is the worst case scenario. You likely paid a premium for the value of that lease, which is now diminishing the asset's value. As part of an acquisition, a reputable sponsor will interview tenants in an effort to handicap the likelihood that each tenant will perform on its existing lease and renew upon expiration.

Operators who are adept at analyzing the quality of a tenant rent roll and assessing rollover risk can create asset value.

Leasing risk: In an asset where current vacancy exists that the sponsor expects to lease up over time, there is risk that the lease up may not occur or may occur at a slower rate than the sponsor anticipates. Good sponsors mitigate lease up risk by budgeting appropriate amounts of time and resources (monetary and human) in a pro forma when contemplating lease up scenarios.

Physical asset risk: There is the potential that unexpected costs may arise due to the condition of the property itself. Aging assets tend to have more risk for unforeseen problems to surface, such as costly roof replacements or equipment failure. Sponsors can mitigate physical asset risk through professional third party reports that examine the physical aspects of an asset and highlight abnormal costs. Good sponsors then utilize these reports to further mitigate risk through renegotiation of price or terms with sellers.

Entitlement risk (new development only): New developments must navigate a lengthy and often complex process in order to obtain municipal approval to construct the project. This is referred to as the entitlement process and, prior to receipt of construction permits, all new development possess entitlement risk. Since this process is detailed and contains many unique features, we have dedicated a chapter to its discussion, "The Real Estate Development Process: Understanding the Risks and Milestones".

Construction risk: Any time a project entails significant construction (new development or redevelopment of an existing asset) there are risks that the construction project may incur cost overruns, take longer than anticipated to complete (creating leasing risk as noted above) or expose previously unknown defects in the physical asset (see physical asset risk above). When looking to invest in a project with significant construction, it's critical that the sponsor have experience in managing construction projects.

Market risk: Real estate as a whole is known for its up and down market cycles. Good markets are characterized by strong occupancies and steady rent growth while downturns often result in lower occupancies and flat or even discounted rents. There are myriad market risk factors that can trigger an imbalance in the supply and demand for space, such as a surge in new development or a dip in demand from a slowing economy.

Geographic risk: Properties are heavily influenced by their location based on the regional, state, city or even a specific neighborhood. Job growth, population and demographics are some of the key ingredients to that equation. Primary markets such as New York, San Francisco, L.A. or Chicago have larger, more diverse economies and a bigger population base to insulate it from market downturns. In contrast, secondary markets are viewed as riskier and tertiary markets as riskier still because they are more susceptible to dips in the economy and have shallower pools of buyers. While primary markets to enjoy the greatest amount of transaction activity, it is also imperative to remain cognizant of this factor becoming overpriced into assets. For example, after an amazing run over the previous five years, core located assets in San Francisco are currently of topic when it comes to the conversation of location overpricing.

Given the discussion of the risks summarized above, it becomes easier to now understand how two real estate investments that both offer the same targeted return may have dramatically different risk profiles. In that regard, it is important for the investor to peel back the different layers of risk to determine the superior risk-adjusted return, which is another way of asking which deal poses the opportunity to earn the most return for the least amount of incurred risk.

One final point is that risk is subjective. Two different investors may have entirely different views of the risks that can translate into different perceived risk-adjusted returns. For example, in the category of tenant risk, one investor may argue in favor of the certainty associated with a single tenant while another investor may argue in favor of a multi-tenant property, citing the huge risk of absolute vacancy if the single tenant vacates - they are both correct.

Investors must make their own judgement calls on risk based upon what feels acceptable in the eye of the beholder. Once a determination of risk level is identified in an investment opportunity, the investor may now proceed with a rational assessment of the deal, which will serve both investor and sponsor well in the event that those risks avail themselves during the holding period.

Leverage: The Double-edged Sword of Real Estate Finance

Leverage, or debt financing, is an important and even necessary part of most real estate deals. However, as the 2008 - 2009 real estate downturn highlighted, there are times when too much leverage on an asset can be a recipe for heavy losses. So, it is important for investors to understand leverage, the pros and cons of using it, what amount of leverage is prudent in a given situation and how it can influence the risk and reward of real estate investments.

Leverage, or debt financing, is an important and even necessary part of most real estate deals. However, as the 2008 - 2009 real estate downturn highlighted, there are times when too much leverage on an asset can be a recipe for heavy losses. So, it is important for investors to understand leverage, the pros and cons of using it, what amount of leverage is prudent in a given situation and how it can influence the risk and reward of real estate investments.

What is leverage?

Leverage refers to the total amount of debt financing on a property relative to its current market value. Loan-to-value ratio is another commonly used term when discussing leverage. However, loan-to-value ratio refers to the amount of a single loan, such as a mortgage as a percentage of the value of a property. Leverage includes all of the different layers of debt in the capital stack, such as first and second mortgages and mezzanine financing. For example, a $10 million office building that has a $7 million mortgage and a $1 million mezzanine loan would carry 80% of total leverage.

> "Leverage is a great weapon for enhancing returns when wielded appropriately. In this section, I introduce the concept of "prudent" leverage. Understanding prudent leverage requires the use of debt coverage service ratios, which I cover in the next section."
>
> Ian Formigle

The Upside of Leverage

Real estate owners and developers often rely on leverage as a means to increase the potential return on an investment. The reason that leverage increases returns on a property is because the cost of debt financing, such as a bank loan, is usually cheaper than the unleveraged returns a property can generate. By inserting leverage, you can take the additional return from the leveraged portion of the project and apply it to the remaining equity to enhance leveraged returns. In simple terms, leverage allows investors to get substantially more bang for the buck.

For example, one investor has $1 million in equity to invest and he decides to put 50% leverage on a property, which allows him to buy a $2 million retail building. A second investor has the same $1 million to invest, but she decides to use 75% leverage to buy a $4 million office building. From a capital stack perspective (for more details see our previous chapter, "Understanding the Capital Stack") the two deals look like this:

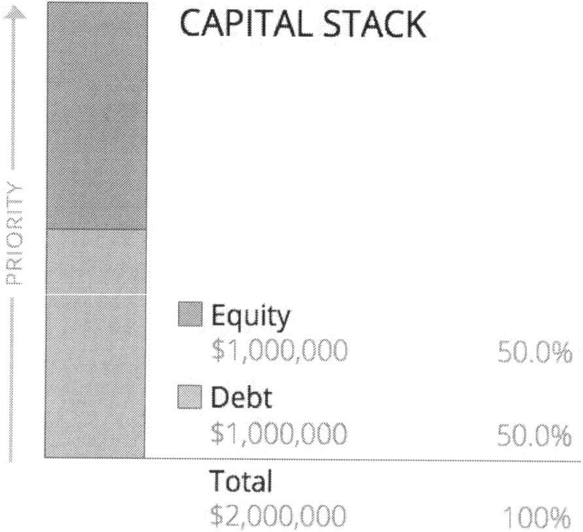

In the first year, both properties appreciate by 10% and both investors decide to sell. Even though the two investors had the same amount of equity to start and both experienced the same percentage of property appreciation, the first investor makes a gross profit of $200,000 on the transaction while the second investor makes a gross profit of $400,000. This discrepancy in profits highlights the power of leverage in generating returns, assuming that things go well. The potential for this type of additional upside creates a strong incentive for investors to utilize higher leverage, sometimes as much as can be obtained.

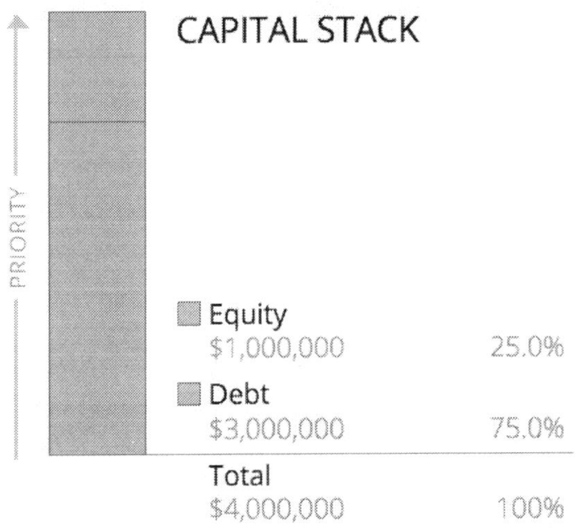

How much Leverage is Prudent?

In some cases, higher leverage can translate to higher risk. For example, there were plenty of three to five-year loans issued from 2005 to 2007, just prior to the recession at high leverage amounts of 85% to 90% of acquisition value. Adding to that risk is the fact that those loans were based off of what we now know were peak property values.

So, when the market shifted and property values dropped precipitously in 2008 to 2009, those borrowers found themselves underwater in the properties right at the point their debt matured. Similar to what happened in the housing market, certain borrowers found themselves in predicaments where the outstanding mortgage balances were higher than what the properties were now worth. When confronted with these situations, the only way to retain the assets was to de-leverage them or place new smaller mortgages on the properties (and even this was nearly impossible given the illiquidity at that time) and pay off the balance of the existing mortgages with newly infused equity. Tragically, the solution for many owners was to hand the keys back to the bank and walk away from debt-burdened properties.

While the overuse of leverage was the culprit of many failed deals during the financial crisis, the risk of high leverage can be mitigated through certainty of execution. For example, if a sponsor has a building that is fully leased to a stellar credit tenant such as Amazon on a long-term lease, it is reasonable to place a high level of leverage on such a property knowing that Amazon would have to go out of business before it stopped paying rent. In contrast, if a sponsor has a dozen tenants in a building, all of which are small mom and pop businesses on short-term leases, the safer play is to be more conservative on leverage knowing that the exposure to future vacancy, and hence lower income from the property, is remarkably greater.

Investors can analyze leverage as another metric to gauge the risk versus potential returns of real estate projects when making investment decisions. For example, when comparing one deal with a 16% Internal Rate of Return or "IRR" and low leverage with another deal that targets a 19% IRR but with high leverage, the lower IRR deal may actually be more favorable because the the additional 300 basis points difference in targeted IRR may not adequately compensate the investor for the higher financing risk. This is what is referred to as "risk-adjusted returns".

The Use of Leverage in the Current Cycle

While the downturn in the commercial real estate market in 2008 and 2009 produced some harsh lessons on leverage for certain owners, it has also spawned opportunities for investors in the current cycle. The subsequent deleveraging of commercial real estate in the aftermath of the downturn has created a need for higher percentages of equity in capital formation. This shift to the use of greater amounts of equity has helped propel growth for real estate investing platforms such as CrowdStreet. Despite the post-recession recovery, some lenders remain relatively conservative and, as a result, lower levels of leverage are more the norm, perhaps for good reason. That has created opportunities for real estate investors to fill that financing gap via both equity and debt real estate investments. CrowdStreet offers both debt and equity investment offerings on its CrowdStreet Marketplace.

Assessing Real Estate Investment Risk Using Debt Service Coverage Ratios

Real estate investors can reach into a lender's toolkit to help them assess potential real estate investments. One tool, the Debt Service Coverage Ratio (DSCR), is a common metric lenders use to underwrite real estate loans. It is a measure of the projected cash flow available to pay debt obligations on the property's real estate loan. In this article, we will describe DSCRs and explore how they can be used in conjunction with other metrics, such as IRRs to provide more insight on risks relative to returns in comparable assets.

Lenders use DSCRs to determine whether or not they will issue loan terms to borrowers and, assuming they do, they then use DSCRs to size loans. They also use DSCRs to assess risk and determine fees and interest rates they charge on loans. Since lenders use DSCRs to size up a deal, investors can also use this metric to compare and contrast different investment opportunities.

If the annual net operating income of a property is $3 million and the annual debt service is $2 million, then the DSCR is 1.5. So what does that number mean? For starters, it means that the property can suffer a $1 million decline in NOI and still service its debt. It also means that beyond a $1 million decline in NOI, the property drops below a 1.0 DSCR, which is an important number. A DSCR below 1.0 is bad as it means a property no longer has enough net operating income to service its debt. Furthermore, if a property drops below a 1.0 DSCR for a prolonged period of time without an immediate path to get back above that threshold, then the probability of the borrower defaulting on the loan increases substantially. Therefore, the closer you get to a 1.0 DSCR, the more lenders become nervous as unexpected hits to revenues (such as a vacancy or a tenant default) or increases to operating expenses could cause a default.

> "The debt coverage service ratio ("DSCR") is a great metric to use to determine whether assets are prudently or overleveraged. In this section, I define the DSCR and provide guidelines for using it to identify risk."
>
> 
>
> Ian Formigle

DSCR Ranges

While there is no absolute standard when it comes to preferred or accepted DSCRs, there are general underwriting guidelines for institutional-quality assets that vary across asset classes. For example, for multifamily assets, agencies such as Fannie Mae or Freddie Mac seek minimum DSCRs of 1.2 or 1.25 (depending upon the asset and amount of leverage sought) when underwriting loans. Given the relative stability of multifamily assets in comparison to other asset classes, lower DSCRs are justifiable. In comparison, if you were underwriting a similar quality stabilized office or retail asset in a similar market, the greater level of tenant risk (e.g. fewer tenants each of whom accounts for a greater percentage of operating revenue) would mandate a higher DSCR, such as 1.5 or greater. Generally speaking, DSCRs can range from below 1.0 (in the case of a heavy value-add deal where you plan to lease up a building with an interest reserve to service the first two years of debt) to upwards of 3.0. While it's possible to have a DSCR above 3.0, particularly if the amount of leverage placed on a property is low, it's rare. For most commercial assets, a DSCR above 2.0 is attractive as it means the property has a good margin of error for unforeseen occurrences that could negatively affect NOI yet still provide enough cashflow to service its debt.

Using the DSCR to understand risk vs. reward

Investors can use DSCRs to better understand the risk in a real estate deal. For example, an investor can use the ratios to compare two apartment investment opportunities in Dallas that, from the outset, appear to have similar profiles in terms of unit counts, asset class and location.

Property A has a DSCR of 1.6 and a targeted IRR of 14%. A relatively high DSCR for a multifamily property means it is more stable and it could withstand sudden changes, such as a 5% drop in occupancy without risk of default. It also means you can expect greater dependable cash flow. By comparing the DSCR to the targeted IRR, we can categorize this asset as Core-plus.

Property B has a DSCR of 1.2 and a targeted IRR of 18%. Based upon the guidelines above, you also know that the sponsor has, at least initially, maximized the amount of available debt. As you learn more, you discover that the sponsor has opted to be more aggressive on debt at acquisition because of a unit improvement plan that will translate into higher rents at lease renewal. Therefore, while the year 1 DSCR is 1.2, the pro forma suggests a DSCR of 1.7 by year 3, which makes sense if the unit improvement plan is implemented. By comparing the initial vs. future DSCR to the targeted IRR, we can now categorize this asset as Value-added.

Debt vs. equity underwriting

Investors sometimes have a tendency to believe that, if a lender is involved in a transaction, then it has been through a rigorous due diligence process that also benefits them. While it is true that lenders conduct substantial due diligence to get comfortable prior to committing to lend on a property (which includes items such as title and survey review, environmental reports and physical inspections), it shouldn't necessarily correlate to equity investors feeling equally comfortable. Investors should keep in mind that the lender has conducted due diligence sufficient to feel comfortable with its downside exposure in the transaction, which might come at the expense of equity investors. The lender may also be willing to take on a bigger loan risk if it is charging a higher fee on the loan. Or, the lender may be willing to assume more risk due to competitive pressure to win the deal. Having a lender in a transaction is good from a checks and balances perspective, but it doesn't mean that investors can outsource their own due diligence.

What are Real Estate Risk-Adjusted Returns?

A risk-adjusted return is a measure that puts returns into context based on the amount of risk involved in an investment. In this chapter we walk you through a detailed process for estimating relative risk-adjusted returns across various commercial real estate investment opportunities. After completing this chapter you should have a better understanding of how risk and returns vary in competing investments, as well as an appreciation of how many times the investment with the highest IRR may not always offer the best risk-adjusted return.

A risk-adjusted return is a measure that puts returns into context based on the amount of risk involved in an investment. It is a common term in the investment world, particularly as it relates to discussing returns on equities and fixed income that is derived utilizing the following equation:

Risk-adjusted return on Capital (RAROC) = Expected Return / Value at Risk

Real estate doesn't offer the same technical analytical approach to measuring risk as can be done in securities analysis. However, the concept the concept is still applied to real estate investment returns.

"Now that you understand the basics of risk and targeted returns, plotting them along a curve provides a comparative analytical tool. In this section, I describe how to calculate a risk-adjusted return and compare two different investments."

Ian Formigle

The first step for investors is to begin with the base concept of risk-free return, which is the theoretical rate of return for zero risk. In the real world, there is no such thing as zero risk, but the closest we get to it is U.S. Treasuries, since the U.S. would need to default on its debt obligations for the investor to not be paid the promised rate of return. To put the risk-free rate of return into the perspective of real estate, it's helpful to align around holding periods. Given that real estate is commonly held for periods that can range from three to seven years, we can look to current U.S. Treasury yields over the same maturity dates (as of May 16, 2016), which range from 0.94% (3-year Treasuries) to 1.55% (7-year Treasuries). Therefore, it's a reasonable starting point to take the midpoint of that range and assume that the risk free rate of return is 1.25%.

Now that we have our risk free starting point, every percentage point of risk beyond a 1.25% annual return incurs risk. In theory, risk and returns have positive correlation, which can be graphed like this:

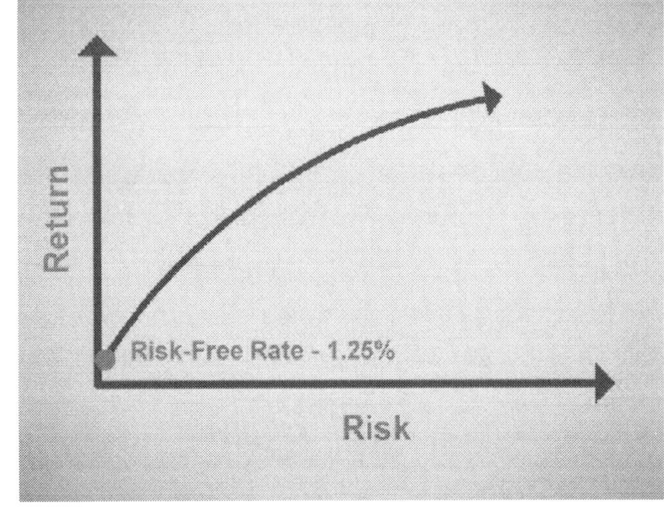

Stepping out on the risk curve generally has a correlation with a higher return. For example, a low-risk core deal, such as buying an unlevered trophy office tower in Manhattan, has the lowest returns. Each incremental step further out on the risk curve – moving to core-plus, value-add and opportunistic investments – should produce a corresponding increase in return. For further discussion on this topic please see "Real Estate Investment Strategy: Four Categories of Risk & Reward".

One way to interpret the risk / reward graph above is that moving out along along the risk / reward line is "fair value" or the appropriate amount of added risk for the corresponding reward. If an investment plots to the right of the line, then it possesses excess risk for the offered return. If it plots to the left of the line the it possesses below fair value risk for offered return:

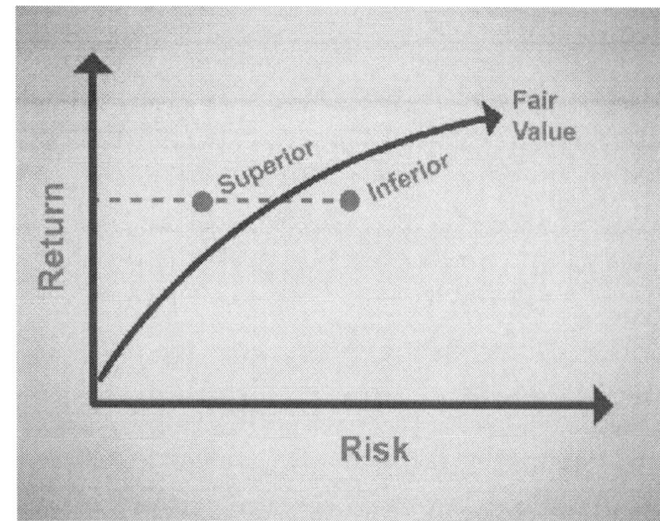

Conversely, if you have two competing investment opportunities that possess the same level of risk but offer different returns, the superior investment will plot above the line and inferior investment below the line:

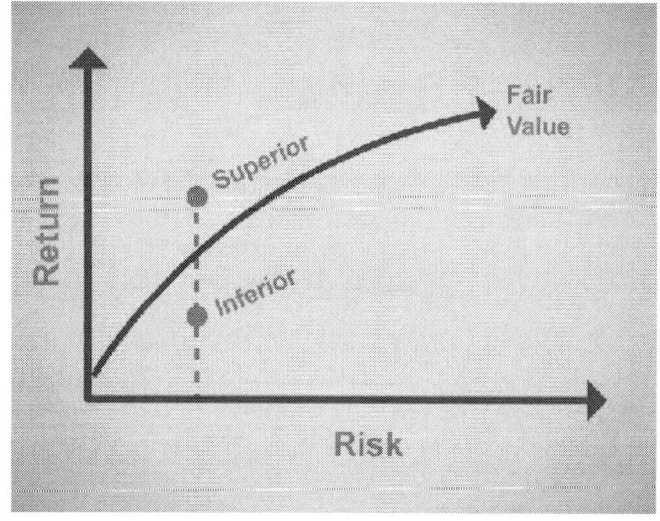

The second graph demonstrates how plotting the returns side of the graph is the easy part; it's the risk side that is nuanced. Therefore, the most efficient way to compare competing investment opportunities is to begin by stacking elements of risk to estimate that piece.

To begin estimating risk, investors must have a basic understanding of the sources of risk in a real estate investment (see: "Top 10 Sources of Risk in Real Estate Investment Deals"). Outside of real estate, there are risk-adjusted return calculations to help determine whether investors are extracting the highest possible gains with minimal risk involved. There are different methodologies to come up with a specific number or ratio, including popular risk adjusted return measures such as Sharpe, Treynor and Jensen's Alpha. In commercial real estate, investors are making a judgement call on perceived risks. It's subjective and depends on the investor's individual tolerance for types of risk within a deal.

As an example consider the following two competing investment opportunities:

	Retail Investment	Office Investment
Asset Type	Grocery-anchored retail shopping center	Office building
Sponsor Experience	Seasoned - 8 years of asset class experience in the subject market	Tenured - 20 years of asset class experience in the subject market
Targeted IRR	14%	16%
Targeted Holding Period	5 years	5 years
Occupancy	95%	80%
Tenant Profile	Grocery anchor is credit tenant on 10 year lease. Remaining tenants are mom and pop operators with average remaining lease term of 4 years.	Multi-tenant. No tenant occupies more than 20% of total leasable space. Average remaining term is 3.5 years.
Construction Vintage	2008	1990
Market	Secondary - suburban	Primary - urban
Leverage	65 LTV	70 LTV

Now that we have two assets to compare, we then, on a scale of 1 to 10, assign a risk score to individual risk categories and sum the score to generate a risk index score. This example is simplistic as it gives equal weight to each category. In addition, it is easy to challenge each category score. The point is to illustrate that it is possible to quantify risk once you have opinions on how to rate individual risk factors. Again, please see "Top 10 Sources of Risk in Real Estate Investment Deals" for more discussion on each risk category:

	Retail Investment	Office Investment	Notes
Sponsorship	5	2	20 years of asset class experience is significant.
Debt	4	6	5% additional leverage exposes asset to greater probability of default in event of spike in vacancy.
Cap Rate	6	4	All things being equal, cap rates tend to expand at a greater rate in secondary vs. primary markets during a downturn.
Tenant	2	7	Having a credit tenant on a 10-year lease is a significant differentiator.
Leasing	3	7	The credit anchor in the retail investment limits leasing risk. The office deal will constantly face it.
Physical Asset	3	6	2008 vs. 1990 is a notable difference. The office building may be facing end of useful life issues with roofs, HVAC, etc.
Market	5	6	Grocery anchored and tenant term gives the nod to the retail investment for market risk.
Geographic	5	2	Urban Primary is notably less risky than Secondary suburban from a geographic standpoint.
Risk Score	33	40	

Now that we have comparative risk scores and known targeted IRRs we can now plot the deals against each other:

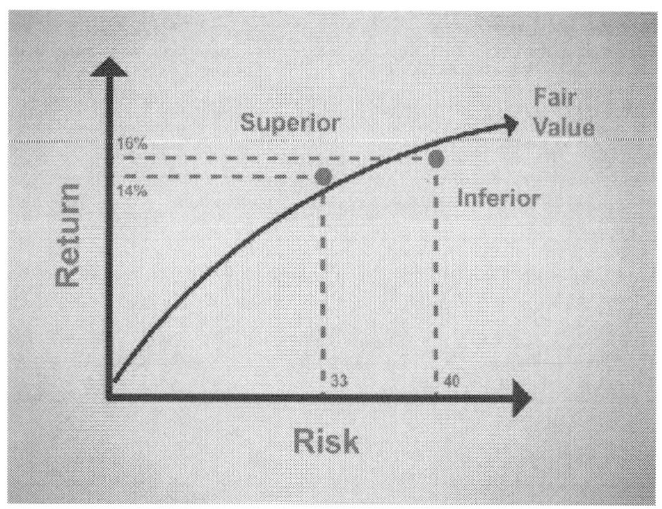

Based upon the graph above, the plot suggests that the retail investment provides a better risk adjusted return. This finding can also be supported by the notion that to receive an additional 14.3% of annual return (14% to 16% IRR) you must incur an additional 21% of risk score (33 to 40). Therefore, provided you feel comfortable with the weighting and score of each risk factor, you now have a basis to claim that the office investment incurs too much additional risk for the return offered.

Now that you have an understanding of how risk and returns can vary in competing investments, you can now appreciate, as highlighted above, how the investment with the highest IRR may not offer the best risk-adjusted return. Ideally, investors are looking for real estate investments that offer better returns for the same amount of risk or the same returns for lower risk.

As a final note, pay attention to how risk may change, and often diminish, in a given investment opportunity as the deal unfolds. For example, throughout due diligence processes, sponsors learn quite a bit about target acquisitions. If a sponsor learns that a roof or HVAC needs replacement, prices that into the pro forma and is able to leverage this knowledge to achieve a pricing discount from the seller, then the investment just decreased in risk with perhaps little to no impact on the IRR. Hence, the risk-adjusted return just improved.

Investors should balance risk and reward in order to attain optimal risk-adjusted returns.

The Real Estate Development Process: Understanding the Risks and Milestones

Real estate development is a multi-step process that can be complicated, lengthy and risky. It can take years to bring a project from the initial planning stage through construction to final completion, and there are plenty of obstacles that can pop up along the way. Yet development projects also can be highly profitable investment opportunities. Through developing an understanding of the life cycle of a development project, investors can more confidently assess some of the risks associated with any potential CRE investment.

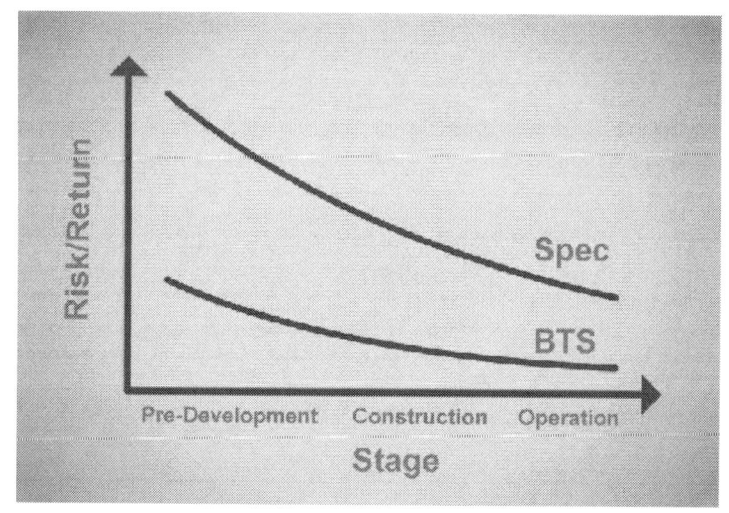

Real estate development is a multi-step process that can be complicated, lengthy and risky. It can take years to bring a project from the initial planning stage through construction to final completion, and there are plenty of obstacles that can pop up along the way. Yet development projects also can be highly profitable investment opportunities. By definition, development projects provide the opportunity to deliver a product that does not currently exist into a market, often providing the fresh new supply to satisfy pent up market demand. When executed well, this aspect of a development project can translate into a runaway success story, something that simply isn't nearly as possible with an existing asset. Investors can more confidently assess

some of the risks associated with construction by better understanding the "life cycle" of a development project.

Risk across project type and stage

Two factors can play a big role in the risk of a given project: the project type and stage. As shown in the graph above, the project type can determine the steepness of the risk curve across the project life cycle.

An example of a project type with relatively low risk across all stages of the life cycle is a retail "build-to-suit" project. In a retail build-to-suit, a developer secures a long-term credit tenant, such as a McDonald's or Walgreens, and develops a property to suit that tenant. For these types of projects, construction risk is low because the buildings are fairly uniform, and leasing risk is almost non-existent because the tenant is already identified and under lease with limited ability to terminate. There may be some pre-development risk depending upon the regulatory hurdles, as described in the Pre-Development section below.

At the opposite end of the spectrum, an example project type with relatively high risk across all stages is called a "speculative" or "spec" project. In a spec industrial or office project, a developer may have few or no leasing commitments before commencing construction. The developer justifies the project by pointing to existing or projected demand for the property after completion. For speculative projects, the leasing risk is high because there are no identified tenants at the outset, the construction risk can be high if the project design is unique, and the pre-development risk can be high if financing is difficult to obtain or regulatory hurdles abound.

As each step in a development project is completed, overall project risk incrementally abates. Early in the cycle there are more potential obstacles and unknowns. As a project nears the "shovel-ready" construction stage, many of those potential obstacles have been addressed and resolved and there is more certainty related to execution, costs and schedule.

Below, we discuss items that are consistent across project types.

Early stage: Pre-Development

The early stage of a project focuses on due diligence, research and permitting. It is often the most variable in duration. Investing at this stage carries the greatest and most varied risks, because there are many unknowns. Some of the common steps in this phase include:

Market analysis and feasibility studies

Land acquisition or securing option rights to purchase land

Environmental assessments

Surveys

Site plans, development plans, and building plans

Permitting

Some infrastructure improvements

Arranging construction financing

Because this stage is the riskiest, pre-development work is usually financed by the project sponsor or a source of seed equity that might get taken out by the construction loan. Investments made during this stage, therefore, provide for higher returns than those made during the later stages. One important note for equity investors is that obtaining construction financing from a bank or other lender is a very rigorous process, and if a developer already has a construction loan arranged, it usually means that a number of major hurdles have been cleared.

"Real estate development is its own animal from a risk perspective. In this section, I describe the three major phases of real estate development and discuss how project risk is reduced with the completion of each phase."

Ian Formigle

Perhaps the greatest impediment to capital formation at this stage is the local jurisdiction permitting. There are usually two distinct approvals required to begin construction: land use approval and building approval.

A land use permit is a governing jurisdiction's approval of the project on a conceptual level. Almost every jurisdiction in the country, with the notable exception of Houston, Texas, has some form of land use regulation, which provides a subject system of sorting and qualifying not only the proposed use of land (retail, industrial, residential, etc.) but also the physical characteristics of the improvements (height, density, setbacks, etc.).

The land use application process can delay a project for months or even years. For this reason, the land use permit, while not the final approval for construction purposes, is often the greatest hurdle to achieve project financing. Some items that might delay land use approval are:

Rezoning process

Appeals from neighbors or other interested parties

Disputes between the developer and the jurisdiction

An involved design process that requires multiple site plan iterations

By granting a building permit, a jurisdiction is approving a project on a technical level. A jurisdiction, through its engineers, will review building plans to determine whether they meet certain safety standards and conform to current building codes. The building permit application process is relatively speedy compared to the land use process because is supposed to be based on objective criteria. For this reason, it is less likely to delay fundraising. The building permit is generally the last milestone in the pre-development stage.

Middle Stage: Construction

The middle stage involves constructing the improvements. Since the pre-development tasks have been completed, the project risks at this stage are greatly reduced but certainly not eliminated. Some of the common steps in this stage include:

- Vertical construction
- Project marketing
- Drawing on construction financing
- Pre-leasing
- Arranging permanent financing (if not done during pre-development)
- Arranging for property manager (if not done during pre-development)

The project typically is financed at this stage by the sponsor, outside investors, and a short-term construction loan. Often, the debt is distributed to the developer in increments called "draws" upon the achievement of construction milestones. Investments and loans made during this stage generally provide lower returns than pre-development investments but higher returns than those made for fully-constructed or stabilized buildings.

The certificate of occupancy generally marks the end of the construction phase and allows for the commencement of property operations. Like the building permit, it is based upon objective criteria regarding construction quality and is a fairly administrative process.

Final Stage: Operation

The final stage of the development process, operation, is the first stage of the building's life. While the pre-development and construction risks may be removed by this point, obtaining tenants is still at risk. Some activities during the final stage include:

- Ongoing marketing and leasing
- Finding a buyer, if not done earlier
- Determining a hold strategy, if not selling
- Ramping up property management
- Achieving stabilization

The project is typically financed at this stage with construction financing or another round of short-term "bridge" financing until the project reaches a threshold called "stabilization," which is typically defined as a certain occupancy level (perhaps 90% or better) for a certain duration (perhaps three consecutive months). Upon stabilization, so-called "permanent" or long-term financing can be placed and used to take out construction financing. Depending upon the amount of pre-leasing that was accomplished during construction, this can be the least risky stage. For this reason, permanent loans and equity investments will provide the lowest returns.

This snapshot view highlights the risk profile of development projects over time; however, many of the same risks applicable to the purchase or refinancing of an existing building, such as sponsor solvency and expertise, economic conditions, and market factors, also apply.

Sources & Uses: Following the Real Estate Money Trail

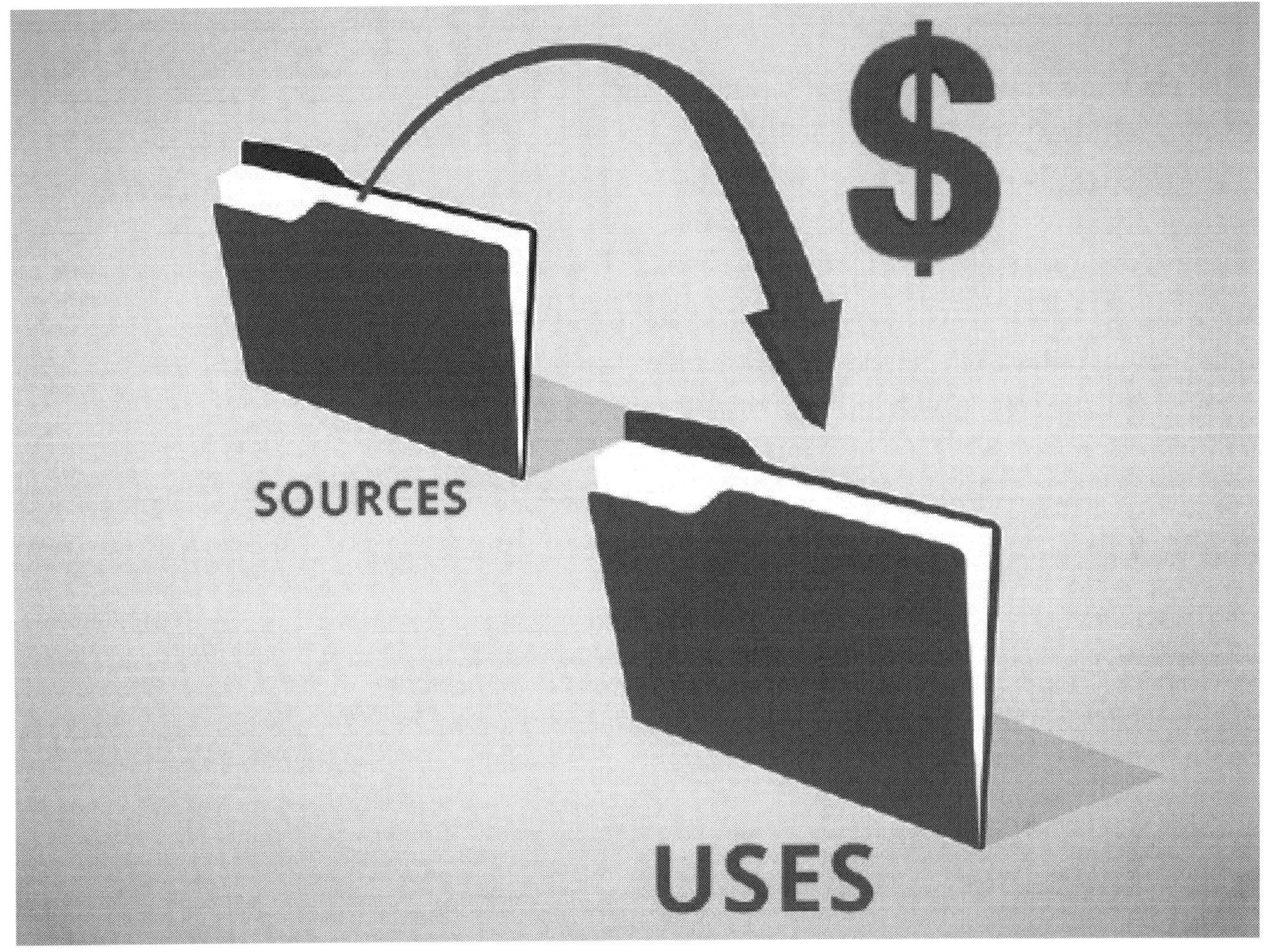

A common resource within real estate pro formas, the Sources & Uses table is intended to serve as a roadmap that shows where project funding comes from (the "Sources of Funds") and how it is to be spent (the "Uses of Funds"). In this chapter, we discuss the constituent parts of the table and how they differ from other investment tools.

Use of Funds

The Uses of Funds detail is a project-level accounting of all project costs across all categories. The Uses of Funds section is derived before the Sources of Funds and dictates how much funding is needed. The sponsor will typically break project costs into price per square foot or per unit, depending upon the property class. The sponsor may also show items as a percentage of overall costs. Although there are myriad ways to group project costs, the most common is to start with three basic categories: purchase price, hard costs, and soft costs. These categories may be broken into line item sub-costs or rolled up in order to simplify the table.

Purchase Price

The purchase price is fairly self-explanatory; it is the price that the operator pays to acquire the land and any improvements, such as buildings and infrastructure. If the land is not being purchased outright as part of the transaction, then it is the price of the lease-hold interest on the building being acquired. Showing the price per square foot here can be useful to show how the cost of acquisition compares to other recent transactions for similarly situated assets.

> "Tracking funds is critical to commercial real estate deals and it begins with the sources and uses. In this section, I describe the components of a sources and uses table and provide examples of some of the key line items."
>
> 
> Ian Formigle

Hard Costs

Hard costs are items that directly improve the property such as construction labor and materials. Sometimes a sponsor will include a hard cost contingency in case of overruns. Again, it can be useful to break these costs into a price-per-square-foot view to get a sense of how competitive the pricing is to the market.

The amount and type of hard costs can provide some insight into the business plan. For example, suppose an investor is comparing two offerings that both carry a total value of $30 million. In the first deal, a sponsor allocates $1 million in hard costs, while in the second the sponsor allocates $12 million to hard costs. The first deal probably is core-plus, with perhaps some deferred maintenance work or pre-funded speculative tenant improvements. The second deal clearly is more of a value-add project with significant property renovation planned.

If the sponsors further break down these costs, the business plan becomes clearer. Suppose the second table is further itemized in two different ways:

Roof Repair	$1,000,000
Replace elevator motors	$,500,000
Plumbing repairs and upgrades	$2,000,000
Seismic Retrofit	$3,000,000
Replace HVAC	$1,500,000
New sprinklers	$2,000,000
Parking garage repairs and improvements	$3,000,000

Total Hard Costs	$12,000,000

Lobby Renovation	$5,000,000
Hallways	$1,500,000
Landscaping	$1,000,000
Restroom Renovation	$1,000,000
Tenant Improvements	$1,500,000
IT Systems	$500,000
Ceilings/Lighting	$1,000,000
Total Hard Costs	$12,000,000

Notice that the first table shows improvements to mechanical systems, roof repairs, seismic improvements and parking garage repairs. This suggests that property has substantial deferred maintenance that the sponsor needs to address in order to catch the property back up to current market standards and retain tenants. Alternatively, the second table allocates significant funding to speculative improvements to interior common areas and landscaping and then allocates funds towards funding future tenant improvements. The second table of uses is likely intended to entice new tenants to lease space at the property at the best prevailing market rates.

Soft Costs

Soft costs are costs associated with the project but that do not provide tangible improvement value. This category is the most varied and include but are not limited to:

Purchase closing costs

Leasing commissions

Legal fees

Organizational fees

Loan acquisition costs

Capital broker commissions

Interest reserves

Equity reserves

It is less useful to show soft costs on a square footage basis, but showing the proportion of soft costs to total project costs can help give a sense of the efficiency with which a sponsor is executing a business plan. In addition, the amount of reserves (both interest and equity) can provide insight into the amount of uncertainty in the execution of the business plan. In general, the more uncertainty the higher the reserves.

Sources of Funds

The Sources of Funds section of the table will very nearly match the capital stack, but it will have a few key differences. First, while the capital stack will show the capital providers for a project and their relative order of repayment priority, the Sources of Funds section takes a deeper dive to show all of the sources of funds in a deal in addition to capital providers. One item that may be listed as a source of funds is operational cash flow. Ground-up development and capital improvement programs can take a long time to complete. Often, the operator can rent a portion of a property while making improvements to another. So, while a portion of the improvements may be funded by investor dollars, a portion may be funded by rents in order to reduce up-front capital needs. However, the Uses of Funds must match the Sources of Funds, so the sponsor will need to include these cash flows in the table.

Another detail that the Sources of Funds section adds is the fund timing. Some funds go to work at closing, while others may be held in escrow to pay taxes or insurance. Cash flow, for example, is one source that is usually put to work on future expenses rather than immediately at closing. Additionally, a sponsor may break down the debt into the initial funding and future funding to be drawn as needed. The capital stack, however, would simply show the total debt irrespective of timing. This can provide a particularly helpful distinction because, often times, future funding of debt is contingent upon certain events that are anticipated but not necessarily known to occur. Therefore, in this situation, the actual amount of debt may end up settling at an amount that is different that what is depicted in the capital stack. Understanding the debt sources will give you a sense of both the initial and future funding, which will translate into the final amount of debt.

As the Sources of Funds section becomes more complex, it becomes more likely that the project itself will be complex and will require an experienced sponsor to successfully carry it out.

What's the takeaway for investors?

The Sources & Uses table is not intended to provide forensic accounting. Instead, it helps to provide a funding road map for how the funds will be raised and how they will then be spent in a project. It is perhaps the single best tool for a quick understanding of a project's particular business model and the expertise it will require to carry out. For these reasons, CrowdStreet will always display a Sources & Uses table on the detail page of its Marketplace offerings.

What Your Portfolio is Missing if you Invest Through Wealthfront or Betterment

Wealthfront and Betterment are disrupting financial services by bringing automated versions of sophisticated investment portfolio strategies to the masses. While powerful tools, these robo-trading platforms are missing the top-performing asset class of the last 20 years, direct investment real estate. In this chapter we outline how smart investors are supplementing robo-trading accounts with $10,000 minimum crowdfunding, direct real estate investments to build truly diversified portfolios.

Platforms such as Wealthfront and Betterment are bringing the the same advanced investment portfolio strategy to the masses (at least a roboticized version of it) that is employed by some of the world's most sophisticated investors (see Invest like Harvard: the benefits of direct real estate investing). By harnessing powerful technology to a rich user experience, it's easy to understand how these two companies, in just a few short years, have amassed $2.6 billion and over $3 billion in assets under management respectively.

In the past, individual investors needed a sizable portfolio to catch the eye - and personal attention - of an asset management team willing to craft an investment portfolio tailored to their own unique requirements. Smaller investors that didn't measure up often found themselves shut out of the managed portfolio approach. Rather, they were left to fend for themselves to choose amongst a sea of mutual funds and stocks through online brokerages such as E*TRADE or TD Ameritrade. Tech-fueled platforms have disrupted this space by giving retail investors the ability to allocate funds across multiple asset classes and even rebalance portfolios in conjunction with the managed portfolio approach. According to Betterment, this methodology can deliver a 4.30% higher annual return than a typical DIY investor.

Kudos to Wealthfront and Betterment for leveraging technology to bring the managed investment portfolio approach and application of modern portfolio theory to retail investors. However, if you think that these platforms offer a one-stop-shop for investing, you are mistaken. What investors are missing out on when they utilize these platforms is the opportunity to add direct real estate investments to the mix. Modern Portfolio Theory advises a target range of 10% to 20% in hard real estate assets for well-diversified portfolios. Wealthfront and Betterment may lay claims to real estate exposure through Vanguard's VNQ but this is a REIT ETF and traditional REIT's are not direct real estate investments. If you invest in a traditional REIT you are purchasing shares of the landlord not the physical asset, which at best, is a derivative to direct real estate that carries with it correlation to equities markets.

Historical results show diversification into direct real estate investments to be effective in posting above-market returns in both up and down market cycles. One notable example of those alpha results is Harvard University's fiscal 2015 performance for its $37.6 billion endowment. Harvard's real estate investments generated the highest returns in its entire portfolio last year at 19.4%. More specifically, the direct real estate investment program generated even higher returns of 35.5%.

> "Portfolio diversification begins with adding commercial real estate to your overall portfolio. In this section, I explain how robo advisor portfolios fail to offer this key component of well-diversified portfolio."
>
> 
>
> Ian Formigle

Investors must look elsewhere to find real estate investments to layer on top of robo advisors and they can do that easily via online real estate investing. Real estate crowdfunding has opened up direct real estate investing to the masses by giving investors access to private offerings at a significantly lower buy-in cost. Platforms such as the CrowdStreet Marketplace leverage technology in much the same way as Wealthfront and Betterment to bring institutional-quality investment opportunities with best-in-class sponsors directly to investors.

Traditionally, to the extent that individual investors participated in direct real estate investment, it has been through exclusive private partnerships. The offline mode of direct real estate investing has highly limited visibility and requires sizable capital commitments to get a seat at the table. For example, most partnerships require a minimum buy-in amount of $100,000 or greater.

The CrowdStreet Marketplace allows investors to access direct real estate investment opportunities at investment amounts as low as $10,000. These new lower minimums allow investors to split up their investment dollars across more investment opportunities to create greater diversification and, according to Modern Portfolio Theory, move closer to the efficient frontier.

For example, instead of placing $100,000 into one deal, an investor can spread that risk out into five or 10 different investments. In that regard, the CrowdStreet Marketplace helps investors build a direct real estate investment portfolio in much the same way they use Wealthfront and Betterment to create their online investment portfolio in stocks and bonds. The CrowdStreet Marketplace gives investors transparent information on a variety of private real estate offerings across the country, as well as provides tools to help investors track performance and manage their real estate asset allocations.

While allocating capital to a solution such as Wealthfront or Betterment is a great starting point, think through the return enhancing investment options available to you, such as direct real estate, and build a truly diversified portfolio - lest you risk becoming the "robo client" of the robo advisor.

The CrowdStreet Marketplace makes direct commercial real estate easily accessible to accredited investors. The platform gives investors the opportunity to diversify their portfolio by providing transparent information on a variety of commercial real estate investment opportunities across the country, as well as providing tools to help investors track performance and manage their growing real estate investment portfolios.

How to Build a Diversified Real Estate Portfolio Using Crowdfunded Real Estate

Diversification is a core principle of portfolio management to minimize risk and achieve a higher overall blended return. Modern Portfolio Theory advocates a 10% - 20% allocation into hard assets such as real estate as a means to increase returns while also lowering risk. However, the principle of diversification doesn't stop at the point of a real estate allocation; it also applies within the real estate allocation itself. Diversifying within a real estate portfolio is easily achievable but it requires an understanding of the different "levers" you can pull to generate it. In this chapter, we explore those levers and highlight the various ways to pull them to assemble a well-diversified real estate portfolio.

Diversification is a core principle of portfolio management to minimize risk and achieve a higher overall blended return. Additionally, as part of a diversified portfolio, Modern Portfolio Theory advocates a 10% - 20% allocation into hard assets such as real estate (see our previous chapter, "Invest like Harvard: The Advantages of Direct Real Estate Investing") as a means to increase returns while also lowering risk, a concept that is referred to as moving closer to the efficient frontier. However, the principle of diversification doesn't stop at the point of a real estate allocation; it also applies within the real estate allocation itself. Diversifying within a real estate portfolio is easily achievable but it requires an understanding of the different "levers" you can pull to generate it.

Categories of risk components

"Once you begin investing in commercial real estate, it's time to begin diversifying within the real estate portion of your portfolio as you add follow on investments. In this section, I walk you through some of the primary "levers" to pull to generate diversification."

Ian Formigle

The first step in building a diversified real estate portfolio is to understand the many different real estate strategy buckets. Investors can spread out risk by making allocations across those categories.

Geography: Location can be defined by a neighborhood, city, state, region or country. It also can be defined by the general size of the market, such as a primary or gateway markets, such as New York, San Francisco or Los Angeles, secondary markets such as Denver, Portland or Austin and smaller tertiary markets. You can mix all of these to create diversification.

Asset Class: Major asset class types include: office, retail, industrial, multifamily, hospitality, senior housing and storage. Real estate markets are cyclical with periodic ups and downs that can affect all asset classes or can affect some classes more and others less. One way to diversify against cyclical risk is by investing across asset classes.

Risk Profile: The risk of a project generally falls into one of four categories starting with low-risk, stable core investments known as "core" strategies and progressing further out on the risk curve to core-plus, value-added and opportunistic at the far end with the highest risk. For more details see our chapter, "Real Estate Investment Strategy: Four Categories of Risk & Reward". When investing in real estate be wary of simply chasing the highest returns and ending up with a portfolio of highly risky real estate assets that can depend on speculative business plans. Smart investors know that not all IRRs are created equal.

Income vs. Equity Multiple: Some properties generate steady, predictable cash flow, while other investments target upside at exit at the expense of little or even no yield or distributions until the property is sold. To create diversification blend income producing opportunities with equity multiple driven ones.

Debt vs Equity: Investors can invest at different points in the capital stack on a real estate deal. Debt and equity deals have very different characteristics and come with different risk and return expectations (for more details see our chapter, "Debt Fund Investing 101"). Some investors may favor one over another, while others choose to place capital in both debt and equity deals. By investing up and down the capital stack you can diversify risk.

Sponsorship: Some investors are comfortable building a long-term relationship with one sponsor, while others may prefer to spread holdings among different developers, operators or capital providers. Others yet still, prefer to invest with multiple sponsors for a period of time and then re-invest with a select few after narrowing the field through experience. By diversifying across multiple sponsors you limit risks associated with sponsorship concentration. Finally, keep in mind that a tenured sponsor has learned many lessons over the years and uses this information to protect investors. Less experienced sponsors may be more error prone but also may offer better terms to investors to compensate for their lack of comparative experience. These aspects make for good reasons to invest with different types of sponsors.

Holding Period: Short-term holding periods offer better certainty from a real estate cycle perspective but also intensify time risk since the business plan must unfold rapidly in order to hit targets. It is also more difficult to generate substantial equity multiples (for more details see our chapter, "The Yin and Yang of Equity Multiples and IRR"). Mid-term holding periods reduce time intensity risk but might bump up against the end of a cycle. Long-term holding periods reduce both of these risks but also typically bring lower targeted annualized returns. Blending different holding periods helps to ensure you eliminate the possibility of having all of your exits come at the same time and potentially "wrong" time. Even in good times, exiting your holdings at the same time presents re-investment risk.

Business Model: Each deal usually has its own unique business plan or strategy, such as a new development, a long-term hold intended to clip a steady coupon or a value-added scenario with small cash flow but predominantly back end loaded. When investing, blend your strategies.

Eating My Own "Dog Food"

It is easy for investors to get blinded by targeted returns and pick deals solely based on the highest displayed numbers. However, as investors expand portfolios, it is important to take a thoughtful approach to selecting real estate investments. As an illustrative example, I myself, am a case study in creating a diversified real estate portfolio through multiple crowdfunded real estate investments. To date, I have personally invested in four CrowdStreet offerings. Here's a summary of those deals:

	Asset Class	Strategy	Location	Sponsor	Business Model
Investment 1	Hospitality	Core-Plus	Tertiary / Midwest	Unique	High cash flow
Investment 2	Office	Value-Added	Primary / West	Unique	Some cash flow with equity upside
Investment 3	Medical Office	Core-Plus	Secondary / Midwest	Unique	Cash flow with equity upside
Investment 4	Multifamily	Develop - to - Core	Secondary / West	Unique	No cash flow initially - then partial return of capital with cash yield on residual capital

As I continue to build my own real estate portfolio, I will further look to further diversify through additional asset classes (e.g. retail and industrial), geography (e.g. East and South) and I may look to invest in debt since, to date, I have invested exclusively in equity.

Create Your Own Strategy

There is no one-size-fits-all strategy to diversification and my version, noted above, is simply one example. Investors might diversify assets across two or three different categories or they may choose to build in multiple layers of diversification. Some investors focus on one investment strategy, such as investing only in a single asset type that they know and understand. Other investors are strictly "core" investors and only invest in stable properties in gateway markets. Regardless of individual preferences, investors can still find ways to diversify even within narrowly defined investment parameters. Core investors can invest in different cities, such as New York, Chicago or Los Angeles, or they can invest in different types of properties in one city, such as an office building, hotel or apartment.

To get started in commercial real estate investing, my advice has always been to start with a particular opportunity that is compelling to you and, at least initially, not to worry about the categories of diversification. Once you have your starting point identified, begin to pull the levers of diversification as you add follow on investments.

Leveraging Diversification to Enhance Real Estate Risk-Adjusted Returns

If you ask real estate investors for their ideal returns profile, the answer is the typical best of both worlds of, "high cash flow with high equity upside". While ideal, these types of returns in a single asset are a bit more theoretical than real. Rather than try to find the nearly fictitious scenario that has both high cash flow and upside, you can create the ideal combination through diversification and blended portfolio returns where each individual investment plays to its strengths. This chapter dives into techniques investors can use to diversify based on geography, property type, investment strategy and more in order to deliver a stronger blend of balanced cash flows. We walk readers through a three-property portfolio example which clearly illustrates the principles needed to apply the techniques to their own real estate investment portfolios.

I covered the basics of how to diversify real estate portfolios by pulling the various "levers" of diversification in a previous chapter. If you missed that chapter, I recommend reading it first, "How to Build a Diversified Real Estate Portfolio". In this chapter, we conduct an exercise that illustrates just how diversification can be utilized to enhance blended risk-adjusted portfolio returns (for a discussion on risk-adjusted returns, see our chapter, "What are Real Estate Risk-adjusted Returns?").

As I discussed in our previous chapter, "Invest like Harvard: The Advantages of Direct Real Estate Investing", Modern Portfolio Theory recommends investing across multiple asset classes with up to 20% of a well-diversified portfolio invested in hard real estate assets. However, the principle of diversification doesn't stop at the point of a real estate allocation; it also applies within the real estate allocation itself. Diversifying real estate portfolios helps to hedge against risks. There are a number of ways to diversify real estate portfolios based on geography, property type and investment strategy to name just a few. That diversification allows investors to create a stronger blend of balanced cash flows.

"Now that you have been introduced to the "levers" of diversification, I explain how to optimize risk-adjusted returns through its use in assembling a portfolio."

Ian Formigle

Think of it this way - if you ask real estate investors for their ideal returns profile, the answer is the typical best of both worlds of, "cash flow with equity upside". While ideal, those types of returns in a single asset are a bit more theoretical than real. High cash flow deals often deliver dependable cash flow at the expense of equity upside while high equity multiple deals often deliver the substantial equity upside at the expense of annual cash flow. Therefore, rather than try to find the nearly fictitious scenario that has both cash flow and upside, you can create the ideal combination through blended portfolio returns where each individual investment plays to its strengths.

To illustrate the point, we will use a hypothetical portfolio. In the following exercise, we will assemble a three property portfolio that demonstrates how a combination of strong cash flow with an attractive overall targeted IRR is achievable. For the sake of simplicity, we will invest a total of $300,000 with $100,000 allocated into three assets with the following profiles:

Amount	Asset Type	Structure	Targeted IRR	Equity / Debt Multiple
$100,000	Stabilized Retail Center	Mezzanine Debt	10%	1.5x
$100,000	Value-added Office	Pref Equity 13.4	13.40%	1.75x
$100,000	Multifamily Development	JV Equity	22.40%	2.67x

Stabilized Retail Center

The first investment is a five-year mezzanine note in a high-occupancy, high-cash flowing shopping center with long-term leases and an anchor tenant. Such an asset provides enough certainty of cash flow that it can withstand the additional leverage of mezzanine debt. A mezzanine debt investment will typically offer a high yield but little to no upside at exit. This investment offers a simple 10% yield, interest only, paid monthly over the term. While a mezzanine loan is subordinate to a senior loan, since it is still debt, the annual yield must be paid monthly on time by the borrower. If the borrower fails to pay the mezzanine note then it defaults, which then empowers the investor to take corrective actions that can include foreclosing out the subordinate equity position. Due to these factors, the cash flow from the mezzanine loan is the most secure of the three investments in the hypothetical portfolio.

	Initial Investment	**Year 1**	**Year 2**	**Year 3**	**Year 4**	**Year 5**
Investment / Return of Principal	($100,000)					$100,000
Annual Yield		$10,000	$10,000	$10,000	$10,000	$10,000
Total Cash flow	($100,000)	$10,000	$10,000	$10,000	$10,000	$110,000
Annual Yield		10.00%	10.00%	10.00%	10.00%	10.00%

Avg. Annual Yield	**IRR**	**Investment Multiple**
10.00%	10.00%	1.5x

Value-Added Office

The second investment is preferred equity in a value-added office building. The business plan of this asset is to increase the net operating income on a well-leased office property through substantial rent bumps on a number of leases that roll over the holding period. The investment offers an 8% preferred return and a small profits participation at exit.

While the investment is positioned similarly in the capital stack to the mezzanine debt investment above (i.e. subordinate to a senior loan but ahead of all common equity) payment of the preferred return or annual yield is not compulsory but subject to available cash flow after debt service to the senior loan. That is why it is called a "preferred return". Preferred equity is more suitable in this situation over mezzanine debt because the office property has ongoing tenant lease roll that makes the liability of a fixed obligatory monthly payment above the senior mortgage payment too risky for the equity position. Since the preferred equity incurs that additional risk, it deserves a greater return.

	Initial Investment	Year 1	Year 2	Year 3	Year 4	Year 5
Investment / Return of Principal	($100,000)					$100,000
Preferred Return		$8,000	$8,000	$8,000	$8,000	$8,000
Profits Participation						$35,000
Total Cash Flow	($100,000)	$8,000	$8,000	$8,000	$8,000	$143,000
Annual Yield		8.00%	8.00%	8.00%	8.00%	8.00%

Avg. Annual Yield	IRR	Investment Multiple
8.0%	13.4%	1.75x

Multifamily Development

The third investment is joint venture common equity in a multifamily development situated in an urban location of a secondary market with strong population inflows. This equity investment is subordinate to a construction / mini-permanent loan that is 70% of the total project. Given that the investment a) is ground up development, b) takes first dollar loss risk and c) has no cash flow until the project is constructed and stabilized, it is substantially riskier than the previous two investments. As a result, it should earn the greatest total returns. While high risk, this investment has the potential to deliver an outstanding equity multiple if the business plan is executed as contemplated.

	Initial Investment	Year 1	Year 2	Year 3	Year 4	Year 5
Investment / Return of Principal	($100,000)					$100,000
Cash Yield		$0	$1,250	$8,500	$10,000	$12,000
Profits Participation						$135,000
Total Cash Flow	($100,000)	$0	$1,250	$8,500	$10,000	$247,000
Annual Yield						

Avg. Annual Yield	IRR	Investment Multiple
6.4%	22.4%	2.67x

Blended Returns

If we assemble the three individual investments into a single set of blended portfolio cash flows, this is the result:

	Initial Investment	Year 1	Year 2	Year 3	Year 4	Year 5
Investment / Return of Principal	($300,000)					$300,000
Cash Yield		$18,000	$19,250	$26,500	$28,000	$30,000
Profits Participation						$172,000
Total Cash Flow	($300,000)	$18,000	$19,250	$26,500	$28,000	$502,000
Annual Yield		6.00%	6.40%	8.80%	9.30%	10.00%

Avg. Annual Yield	IRR	Investment Multiple
8.1%	16.1%	1.98x

By diversifying across three investments that have unique asset classes, business plans, structures and sponsors, we end up with a blended average annual yield of 8.1% where the cash flow is predominantly coming from structures that provide greater certainty of delivering that cash flow (mezzanine debt and preferred equity). In addition to the cash flow, the portfolio also targets a 16.1% IRR where the upside is predominantly coming from an asset class and business plan (multifamily development) that is best suited towards delivering substantial equity upside.

What's the takeaway for investors?

Investors can use diversification to build a portfolio that offers a blend of both cash flow and upside. By building a portfolio, you also generate a set of targeted cash flows where the individual components of annual cash flow and back-end upside each have a higher probability of meeting or exceeding expectations since you are creating that blend through more focused investments that play to individual investment strengths. In addition, investors are diversifying away from single event types of risks. So, as a portfolio grows from one asset to two, 10 or even 100, that risk continues to diminish and the probability of a full payment becomes more likely. That, as modern portfolio theory describes it, is moving closer to the efficient frontier.

The CrowdStreet Marketplace makes a point to include a variety of different types of offerings across its platform to help investors build portfolio diversity as they continue to increase their real estate investments. CrowdStreet also provides investors with a single dashboard to track and manage those investments.

The Returns Fallacy: Contemplating Volatility in Real Estate Targeted Returns

The assumption that the path to high realized portfolio returns is simply the sum of a series of high individual targeted returns is a recipe for disaster. Despite this, it is tempting for investors to take information at face value. This is why it is common for less sophisticated investors to fall prey to what I refer to as the "Returns Fallacy". In this chapter we describe the Returns Fallacy and describe techniques investors can use to improve their realized investment returns.

There is a lot more to understanding investment returns in a commercial real estate deal than a quick glance at summary metrics and it starts with targeted returns. The assumption that the path to the high realized portfolio returns is simply the sum of a series of high individual targeted returns is a recipe for disaster. Despite this, it is tempting for investors to take information at face value, because challenging assumptions requires some context. This is why it is common for less sophisticated investors to fall prey to what I refer to as the "Returns Fallacy".

The Returns Fallacy begins with assuming that all deals are created equal and, as a result, simply selecting a portfolio of investments that target the highest returns. A simplistic analysis suggests that a targeted Internal Rate of Return ("IRR") of 20% is better than a 15% targeted IRR, right?

Wrong. When investors select investments based solely on the criteria of a targeted IRRs, they ignore the volatility assumed in achieving those targeted returns. In this chapter, we explore how risk intertwines with targeted IRRs with a focus on volatility of returns.

The four food groups for risk

> "If only investing in commercial real estate were as simple as selecting the highest targeted returns and calling it a day. In this section, I explain why such a practice would be tantamount to falling victim to what I refer to as the 'Returns Fallacy'."
>
> 
> Ian Formigle

In a previous chapter we discussed the four main risk-profile categories in depth. For the purposes of this chapter, I will revisit only the highlights of each category, which represent a sliding scale for risk starting with core strategies as the safest play and gradually stepping out farther on that risk spectrum with opportunistic strategies viewed as the riskiest.

Core properties are relatively stable assets that are typically located in major metros, such as high-rise office towers or apartment buildings in New York City, Chicago or San Francisco. They are best-in-class properties in top locations with high occupancy levels and good credit tenants.

Core plus assets may share many of the same characteristics as core assets with one or more exceptions that create an added layer of risk. Some examples of those exceptions might include the age or condition of the asset, lower tenant credit or a less than stellar location.

Value add assets generally have a problem that needs fixing, such as leasing to improve significant vacancy, building renovation or bringing in new tenants to boost the quality of the rent roll. The purchaser is usually coming in with a specific business plan to improve an underutilized asset.

Opportunistic deals are often extreme turnaround situations. There are major problems to overcome, such as a large vacancy, structural issues or financial distress. Opportunistic strategies may involve acquiring distressed or foreclosed assets from banks or servicers. Alternatively, opportunistic investors may also acquire senior loans of distressed assets at a discount from banks or servicers with a plan to either implement a workout with the existing borrower and sell the loan or take title to the asset via foreclosure on the borrower.

Core vs. Opportunistic Investment Example

Now that we have revisited the four categories of investment risk, let's compare two different office investment examples:

Core Office Deal

Asset Class	A - Trophy
Tenant	Single - Credit
Location	Primary Market - Central Business District ("CBD")
Loan to Value	55%
Current Occupancy	100%
Stabilized Occupancy	95%
Average Remaining Lease Term	15 years
Holding Period	7 years
Targeted Investor IRR	9%

Opportunistic Office Deal

Asset Class	B - Historic
Tenant	Multi-tenant - no credit
Location	Secondary Market - CBD
Loan to Value	65%
Current Occupancy	60%
Stabilized Occupancy	95%
Average Remaining Lease Term	2.5 years
Holding Period	4 years
Targeted Investor IRR	20%

When comparing these two investment choices, it's easy to become seduced by the allure of a targeted 20% IRR and opt for the opportunistic office deal, but is it really better than the core deal? Perhaps, but to make that determination, it is critical to assess the key attributes of each deal and how they affect the likelihood of the asset achieving its targeted returns:

Asset Class - Class A office is superior to Class B office all things equal. In general, it will lease faster and easier than Class B office, which is particularly true in a CBD location.

Property Condition - The better the condition of the asset, the higher the probability that budgeted operating costs will equal actual operating costs and the lower the probability that unforeseen costs will occur.

Tenant Profile - The stronger the tenant, the higher the probability that the tenant performs over the term of its lease. Once tenants reach a AAA credit rating level (such as Microsoft and Johnson & Johnson), their debt is actually considered safer than U.S. Treasury bills and bonds. If you combine tenant credit with term, you essentially have a very safe bond.

Location - Primary markets are considered less risky than secondary markets due to their superior liquidity. International investors will always invest in primary U.S. markets but not always in secondary markets. Sustained international demand for primary markets creates a stronger asset value floor relative to secondary and, especially, tertiary markets.

Loan to Value - The lower the debt amount, the lower the required debt service, which means the lower the probability of defaulting on a debt service requirement and losing the asset to the lender.

Current Occupancy to Stabilized Occupancy - Average Remaining Lease Term - The longer the average remaining term, the lower the amount of lease roll or exposure to risk that current tenants vacate instead of renew their leases. A longer average term creates greater certainty, which limits downside risk, but it also limits upside potential as it locks in lease rates, and thus income, for a longer period of time.

Holding Period - Holding period cuts both ways from a risk perspective. The longer the holding period the more exposure to macroeconomic and real estate cycle risks. Alternatively, the shorter the holding period, the greater the concentration of risk that things need to right within a specific time frame to achieve the business plan. Generally speaking, the further you get into a current cycle, the stronger the argument becomes for longer holding periods since you hedge against the possibility of hitting your exit window during a downturn.

From the information provided above, we now know one critical piece of information:

Example #1 has a much higher probability of hitting its targeted IRR of 10% than Example #2 has of hitting its targeted IRR of 20% or, in other words, Example #1 has much less implied volatility in its targeted returns.

Why?

A Class A trophy asset will have more predictable operating costs than a Class B historic asset. Any building, regardless of its type, becomes more unpredictable with age. A Class B historic asset may experience costly issues with systems such as elevators and HVAC's that are less likely to occur with a newer building.

In the first example, the Core deal doesn't even need to maintain all of its current occupancy to achieve its stabilized goal. In the Opportunistic deal, the operator needs to increase occupancy from 60% to 95% to hit stabilization.

Example #1 has a single credit tenant, while Example #2 relies on multiple non-credit tenants. The risk of a tenant defaulting on its lease is exponentially higher in Example #2.

In addition, with 15 remaining years of average lease term, the Core deal, with its single credit tenant, will almost certainly still be 100% occupied at exit with 8 years of remaining term - enough to command a high exit valuation. The Opportunistic deal has a tremendous amount of uncertainty both in leasing up to a 95% stabilized occupancy as well as exposure of lease roll during the holding period.Example #1 is located in a Primary market, which is generally considered superior to a Secondary market for the reasons noted above.

With a four-year holding period, Example #2 will rely upon a positive leasing environment to hit its occupancy goals and will likely fail to achieve stabilization if a downturn hits inside of the prescribed holding period.

A good way to think about the difference between Example #1 and Example #2 is to view them through a standard deviation to targeted returns graph:

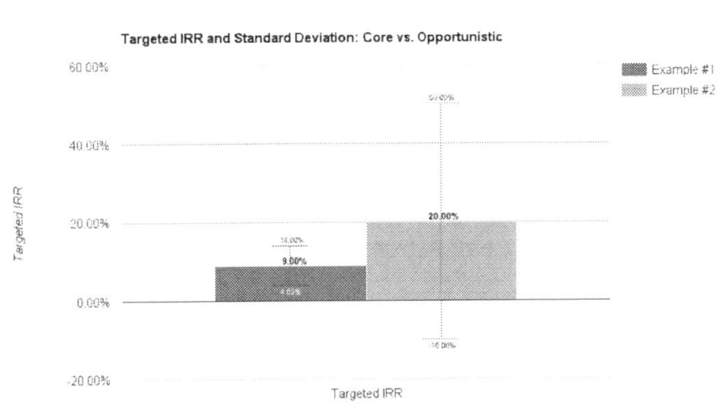

In the graph to right, the blue and grey bars represent the targeted IRRs for the Core Deal (9%) and Opportunistic Deal (20%) respectively. The error bar for each deal represents a one standard deviation variance in each deal's return - 5% for the Core deal and 30% for the Opportunistic deal. The standard deviation in the error bar is a visual representation of the implied volatility of each deal's targeted returns.

Therefore, within a one standard deviation move from each deal's targeted return (which statistically speaking captures 68.2% of probable outcomes) you get the following upside and downside scenarios:

	Downside IRR	Upside IRR
Example #1	4%	14%
Example #2	-10%	50%

In the upside scenario, the Opportunistic deal far out earns the Core deal by a margin of a 36% IRR. However, in the downside scenario, the Core deal still earns a positive return while you take a loss on the Opportunistic deal. What this essentially means is that the Core deal is safe - you can only realistically hope for a 14% IRR but you also have only an outlier chance of losing money. This is the type of deal where you can sleep safely knowing your investment is secure. If capital preservation is paramount, then Example #1 is your deal.

Conversely, the Opportunistic is highly risky - it has huge upside with a 50% IRR but you also lose money within a one standard deviation move to the downside if things don't go according to plan. This type of investment is ideal for high risk capital where you accept the possibility of a loss in exchange for the opportunity to achieve a substantial equity multiple.

So, given the disparity in risk, does this mean that Example #1 is a superior investment to Example #2? Not necessarily. Example #2 may, in fact, be superior to Example #1 in the final analysis. The point is that whether or not Example #1 is a better fit for your portfolio than Example #2 highly depends upon your investment objectives and your tolerance for risk.

Snapshot of risk-adjusted returns

As demonstrated above, risk goes hand-in-hand with the reward or projected return. No investor wants to take on the high risk of a value-add or opportunistic investment only to be compensated at a rate that is more on par with a lower risk core or core-plus deal. While every situation is unique, general guidelines exist to help determine whether the amount of risk for any given deal is commensurate with the targeted amount of return, otherwise known as a risk-adjusted return. Based on data from more than 80 deals offered on the CrowdStreet Marketplace since April of 2014, the following is a snapshot of targeted IRRs for different risk profiles. While by no means an absolute guide, the matrix does provide ranges of actual targeted IRRs with corresponding risk profiles that CrowdStreet determined to as generally commensurate with the amount of assumed risk at the the time the offering was brought to market:

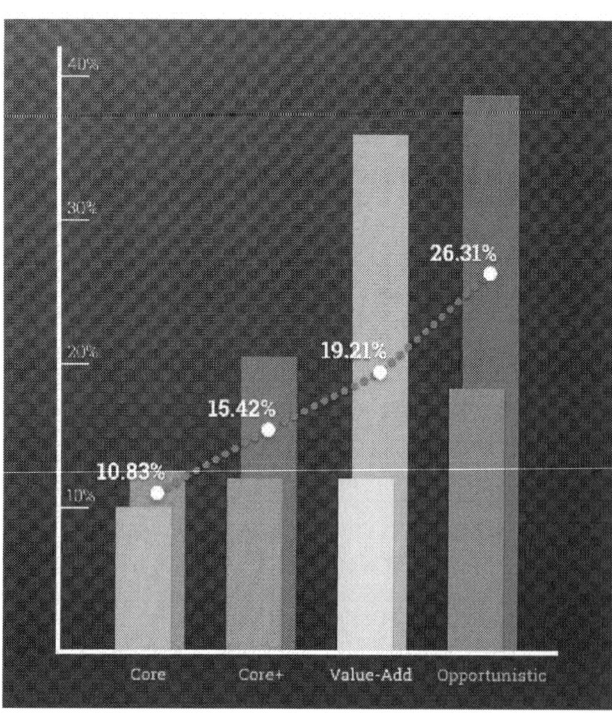

Basic portfolio strategy: Diversify risk

In a perfect world, an investor could simply pick the investment opportunities with the highest IRRs and lock in high returns. However, you now know that such a strategy would only serve to expose that investor to the Returns Fallacy. Diversification is the antidote to Returns Fallacy as it improves overall portfolio returns while also reducing risk - a concept known as moving closer to the efficient frontier. Portfolio diversification can be achieved in a variety of ways, such as investing across property types and geographic markets, as well as with different sponsors and business plans. It also is important to allocate capital across different risk profiles, particularly as we know that commercial real estate is cyclical. That diversification can be especially important in building a portfolio that can withstand a market downturn.

How an investor chooses to weight that diversification depends on an individual's tolerance for risk. It is also important to note that some investors look to commercial real estate as a specific vehicle for taking higher risk to target higher returns and diversify risk through other asset classes such as fixed income. While there are no absolute right or wrong answers when it comes to real estate portfolio diversification, its merits are proven.

The CrowdStreet Marketplace makes a point to include a variety of different types of offerings across its platform to help investors build portfolio diversity as they continue to increase their real estate investments. CrowdStreet also provides investors with a single dashboard to track and manage those investments.

WITH IAN FORMIGLE
VP Investments
CrowdStreet

Thank you for taking the time to learn about CRE Investing and the CrowdStreet investing

To stay up to date on the newest additions to our educational materials, please visit our Investor Center.

To view our latest commercial real estate investment offerings, please visit the CrowdStreet Marketplace.

INFO@CROWDSTREET.COM

610 SW BROADWAY, SUITE 600
PORTLAND, OR 97205
888.432.7693

Get Started in Commercial Real Estate Investing with CrowdStreet, the #1 Direct-to-Investor Marketplace.

Made in the
USA
Lexington, KY

54733405R00087